CHRISTIANITY and SCHOLARSHIP

W. Stanford Reid

The Craig Press

Nutley, N. J.

1966

UNIVERSITY SERIES, *Philosophical Studies*
Dr. Gordon H. Clark, *Editor*

Library of Congress Catalog Card Number 66-21725

Printed in the United States of America

THE AUTHOR

Dr. W. Stanford Reid is the Head of the Department of History at the University of Guelph in Ontario, Canada. Previously, from 1941-1965, he taught in the History Department of McGill University in Montreal, where he was also the Director of Men's Residences.

Dr. Reid received the B.A. and M.A. degrees from McGill University, a Th.B. and Th.M. from the Westminster Theological Seminary, and in 1941 a Ph.D. from the University of Pennsylvania. He is a Fellow of the Royal Society of Arts and of the Royal Commonwealth Society, both of London.

The author of *Church of Scotland in Lower Canada, The Economic History of Great Britain*, and *Problems in Western Intellectual History Since 1500,* Dr. Reid is a frequent contributor to numerous philosophical and historical journals.

CONTENTS

NOTE

Chapters One and Two appeared originally in the *Westminster Theological Journal* and Chapters Three and Four in *The Gordon Review*. The Appendix was first published in *Transactions of the Royal Society of Canada*. Their willingness to grant permission for republication in the University Series is appreciated. Slight revisions have been made in each monograph.

INTRODUCTION

The Christian's engagement in scholarship appears to many non-Christians as a dubious enterprise. If the Christian works within the confines of his faith, how can he be truly scientific? If he would become scientific and engage in an unhampered pursuit of truth, how can he retain his faith in Christian revelation?

Dubious or not, Professor W. Stanford Reid does just that: engage in a Christian scientific enterprise. For some twenty years Professor Reid taught history at McGill University in Montreal and is now Chairman of the History Department at the University of Guelph in Ontario. Having spent much of his career in an academic environment, he has come to know the modern academic mind well. He is convinced that the Christian faith provides a more secure foundation for science than does any humanist version of modern secular thought.

In one sense the Christian's task in scholarship is more difficult than anyone else's. Besides engaging in research, mastering the material of, at least, a part of a particular field, and working with no less vigor than his secular colleagues, the Christian scholar needs to find, in addition, the inner point of connection between the Word of God and his study. But by pursuing this course, his work is more lasting for he contributes to the system of Christian *scientia* on a sure foundation.

In such an enterprise Scripture is more than mere objective communication which the Christian scholar must take into account when he performs his work. In it the voice of the living God speaks to man today and directs him in all his life activities, including his learning. The crying need of the hour is for this dynamic to be worked out in greater detail and significance for the entirety of the scientific enterprise than has been done in the past. The humanist scholar must be shown that he, no less than the Christian, is bound to be the law-structure of creation, and only here will he find a sure footing.

In fact, many Christian scholars need to see this much more clearly than they do.

The chapters of this book were originally articles which appeared in scholarly journals during the past decade. The approach of the author is reminiscent of the views of Herman Dooyeweerd and Cornelius Van Til, of whom Reid is a colleague in learning and in faith. The appearance of this material in its present form will benefit Christian students and scholars alike in their understanding of the Christian's task in learning. Professor Reid has made a significant contribution here. We invite the reader to consider the insights he gives on *Christianity and Scholarship.*

Paul G. Schrotenboer
January, 1966

CHAPTER I

CHRISTIANITY AND SCHOLARSHIP

The word "scholarship," in the twentieth century, has become one of those terms which, like "reason" or "rationality" in the eighteenth century, tend to dominate much of contemporary thought. This is the day of scientific scholarship. Scholars are delving deep into physical nature and human action with the purpose of discovering their meaning and their uses. They are making new and exciting discoveries which are changing not only the pattern of accepted thought, but also the very configuration of our planet. It is this development which the contemporary Christian church, if it would be of much effect in the days to come, has to face and understand. For to scholarship the church may be neither indifferent nor negative. If it would give any guidance to men's thinking in these stirring but confusing times, rather its approach must be positive—an attitude which in the past it has often failed to maintain. To help a little in the clarification of Christian thought on this matter, therefore, the present article is written.

The Present Problem

From the Christian point of view, scientific scholarship has been a great problem for a long time, but only during the past century and a half has this problem become acute. Since 1800 scientific interest and knowledge in the Western world have undergone a continued expansion, for the economic demands and opportunities furnished by the Industrial Revolution have given them an impetus never before known to man. This of itself, however, has not made scholarship a problem. The trouble has been that wherever one has turned one has found that scholarship's assumed basis has usually be naturalism. Most of the leading scientists of both the last and the present centuries: Lamarck, Lyell, Darwin and many others, have consciously based their work on this hypothesis. Of course, there have always been Christians who have been exceptions and some men have claimed to be neutral in their outlook, but to all intents and purposes scientists have generally followed the naturalistic line of reasoning.

Nor have naturalistic presuppositions been limited to the field of natural science. The social sciences have also been brought under their aegis so that history, economics, political science, and sociology are usually studied in a naturalistic context. Even the humanities, with their interest in the activities of man's spirit, which produce poetry, drama, music, and art have been largely forced to bow the knee to the naturalistic "world and life view." One need hardly add that the study of man's mind itself, psychology, has to a large extent been carried along the same road. Thus scholarship, generally speaking, has been founded upon a naturalistic philosophy which claims for itself alone the right to be called "scientific."

Under these circumstances, therefore, it is not surprising that the nineteenth century saw a concerted attempt to bring religion, and particularly Christianity, into conformity with the "universal" assumptions. A very considerable number of the so-called "higher critics" assumed the validity of the naturalistic starting point when they approached the study of the Old Testament. After all, they felt, one can hardly leave the Bible out of this picture; and the result was that before long every effort was devoted to showing that the Old Testament is nothing more than a primitive collection of poorly edited fables, myths, and legends, disguised by a minimum of historical facts as truth. Even here, however, they did not stop, for the next target was the Jesus of the Gospels. "The historical Jesus" became the great quest for New Testament scholars, with the result that before very long they had reduced him to the level, if not below the level, of the nineteenth-century investigator himself. Christianity thus became nothing more than one of the many fields of study for naturalistic scholarship.

The consequence of this development in Western thought has been the growth of the conviction that scientific scholarship and orthodox, supernaturalistic Christianity are incompatible. Indeed, this point of view has so gradually wormed its way into contemporary thinking that to call a man a "fundamentalist" is virtually the same as to say that he believes in witch-burning and that he accepts Bishop Ussher's view that creation took place in 4004 B.C. As one university professor asked of the present writer: "How can one be a believer in the Bible's teaching of supernatural Christianity and still have enough brains to attain a Ph.D. in a social or natural science?" According to most people today, scholarship and true Christian faith simply cannot agree!

Interestingly enough, on this issue the church itself has been divided. There have always been a great many Christians who have had an almost overpowering fear of scholarship. If a man is a scholar, according to their way of thinking, he is already on the broad highway which leads to destruction. Scholarship is evil, leading only to unbelief. Even preachers who show a certain amount of reasoning power, or who wish to approach their work in a scholarly fashion are not infrequently regarded as "unspiritual" and extremely dangerous, while a Christian who becomes a professor, especially in a "neutral" university or college, has reached the point of no return. One might even say that to a good many Christians scholarship is of the Devil.

The reverse of the coin is another common attitude among those who profess to be Christians. It is that Christianity and scholarship are really two mutually separated spheres of knowledge and activity. Nature is there for man's study and interpretation without primary reference to God, although they hold that if the scholar studies nature seriously and logically he will inevitably come to the knowledge that there is a "god" behind all things. The sphere of grace is that in which God deals directly with man through the church for man's salvation. Thus while God is the presupposition of the realm of revelation and grace, for the realm of nature he is but the end-product, and then only in a rather abstract form. This would seem to be the position set forth by Thomas Aquinas in his *Summa Contra Gentiles* and today it largely dominates Roman Catholic thinking.

Some Protestant and even evangelical thinking seems to approximate that of Thomas. Not infrequently one finds some Christians adopting the attitude that scholarship may be divided into two types: that dealing with secular or natural matters and that dealing with revelation. Scholarship dealing with the Christian faith is truly Christian; that dealing with nature, even if it is the scholarship of non-Christians, may also give valid insights into the truth. Man is fundamentally neutral and Christianity may be worked out logically. True, such Christians are by no means entirely consistent in holding this position for they would deny that anyone may become a Christian simply by means of rigorously logical thought. But in dealing with scholarship this is often the approach that they adopt, setting forth what virtually becomes a double way to absolute truth.

Thus many Christians fear scholarship; others desire to ignore it; while others would submit to it. If, however, a Christian is to understand the difference between "naturalistic" scholarship and the Christian interpretation of scholarly activity, he must compare the two and notice their distinctive features. Only then will he be able to see clearly that the non-Christian type of scholarship, which he fears, cannot, by its very nature, be anything but unbelieving. At the same time he must also realize that there is a type of scholarship which is Christian and which leads to the deepening rather than to the destruction of faith. Only when he sees the difference between these two concepts will he be able to appreciate the importance of scholarship for Christianity.

The Differing Concepts of Scholarship

The first difference which is immediately noticeable when one attempts to distinguish between the two types of scholarship is that they have radically different starting points. All thought must begin with assumptions, for man in order to think has to presuppose certain conditions of thought which he cannot prove, either until some time later or perhaps never. In this situation, therefore, the Christian and the non-Christian both find themselves obliged to commence their thinking in the same way: by an act of faith. The similarity, however, proves to be only formal, since their basic assumptions are worlds apart. It is this primary difference which is the reason for the disagreements about everything else, including the nature of scholarship itself.

The non-Christian commences his thinking with the assumption that the universe is a simple "given." Reality "is," and one cannot help but deal with it on that basis alone. The usual eighteenth-century point of view was that the Supreme Being had created the universe and had endowed it with natural laws which would enable it to continue in operation. In the nineteenth century, this point of view fell completely out of favor. Deism was too static, and besides it talked in terms of an original creation. In its place the scientist set forth a dynamic idea of materialistic evolution which operated according to innate laws. This became the starting point of all thought.

The twentieth century has seen the non-Christian's basic presuppositions undergo a somewhat subtle alteration. Materialistic evolution led to a belief in ultimate chance. This seems to have caused a certain amount of concern to many scholars, for if chance be ultimate, the foundation upon which to build any valid interpretation of the universe becomes somewhat unstable. Therefore, there has been a tendency in recent times for a certain segment of non-Christian scholarship to return to the idea of a "God." But these scholars frequently regard their God as limited, to the advantage of an indeterminate evolving universe, and at the same time take for granted the regularity of nature and the autonomy of human reason. One cannot but feel that presuppositions such as these must lead to a certain amount of confusion. Yet despite any possible inconvenience at this point, the non-Christian still takes it for granted that the universe is self-existent.

The Christian on the other hand, commences with very different assumptions. Believing that God, the uncreated, eternal One, is the origin of all temporal reality, he begins with the presupposition of creation. Moreover, he takes this starting point very seriously. All the laws and all the events of the temporal universe are God's. He has established the modal pattern of existence for all things. From this point, in the view of the Christian, should all thought begin, for only here does it commence with the truth.

Yet the Christian would not hold that he presupposes a sovereignly creative God as a belief he had attained by reason. He does so because this God has revealed himself in the Scriptures of the Old and New Testaments. This God being the originator of all things, man should see him and know him by studying the work of his hands. But since man is a sinner whose eyes are naturally and willfully closed to God's sovereignty, he will not see and understand nature as God's creation until and unless God opens his eyes to the true interpretation set forth in the redemptive revelation of the Old and New Testaments. Thus the Christian scholar not only begins by presupposing a sovereign God, but a sovereign God who has revealed himself to men.

It is not surprising, therefore, that self-conscious Christians of all ages have denied that the Bible and nature are in conflict. Rather have they held that they are complementary. Since the universe is God's creation it reveals him by his handiwork; while the Scriptures, on the other hand, being God's Word, show him forth more directly and explicitly, providing the light by which we, although originally blinded by sin, comprehend God's revelation in history. The Christian scholar, therefore, commences all his thinking with the assumption that the sovereign God, set forth in the Scriptures, is the creator and the ultimate interpreter of the universe.

We must, however, go one step further. The Christian scholar does not assume the existence of a God who is merely a mathematical formula or a prehistoric amoeba. Having come to know God in Jesus Christ as his Redeemer, he realizes that he is dealing with an eternal, omnipotent, and omniscient Person. For this reason he is quite prepared to admit that there are many questions to which he may never, even in the next life, know the answers. God acts sovereignly without the need of submitting himself to the will or reason of man. Consequently the Christian scholar commences with the conviction that, while he may try with all his might to understand the universe in which he lives, nevertheless, he must inevitably come to a halt before the sovereign mystery of the Being of God. This is not an attempt to escape from the need of solving problems, nor is it the result of laziness. It is involved in his presupposition itself. Although the universe has been created to be known, limits have been set to man's knowledge of it by God himself through the fact that he made men but finite, temporal creatures.

From the foregoing it should be clear that the Christian and the non-Christian presuppositions are mutually exclusive. While the non-Christian thinks in terms of a self-existent universe, self-existent objects and subjects of knowledge, the Christians hold to a created universe all of whose facts have been divinely interpreted prior to their existence. This divine interpretation the Christian must now, in the light of the Scriptures, endeavor to ascertain, for in this consists his calling to be a prophet, priest, and king unto God.

The differences in the concepts of scholarship, however, go ever further as one sees when one turns to the question of methodology. The non-Christian follows the "objective" method of asking nature, history, and society questions. On the basis of prior knowledge he formulates these questions as hypotheses which he attempts to verify by "experimentation." If the results show the hypothesis to be correct, it is assumed that a new truth has been established; but if the empirical results show the hypothesis to be wrong, another question must be framed in order to find the truth. The scientific, inductive-deductive method has thus become the basic method of science and scholarship. Indeed in the nineteenth century scholars frequently assumed that this was the only way to truth, and that when attained by this means it was new, final, and absolute.

In recent years, however, a change has been taking place. A good many non-Christian scientists have begun to realize that the matter is not quite as simple as it appears. For one thing, hypotheses are not ultimate nor final, but rather are questions limited by the state of one's knowledge, just as Ptolemy's interpretation of the heavens sufficed until empirical knowledge had increased enough to put it out of consideration. Because of this, hypotheses are always controlled by one's presuppositions. Thus the scientific method is not by any means "objective" nor can it be said to have given an ultimate and final answer. Moreover it is not valid in the search for every type of knowledge.

To this conclusion the Christian had come a long time ago. Although he believes the inductive-deductive method of investigation to be decidedly limited in any attempts to achieve a Christian interpretation of God's relationship to his creation, he is nevertheless prepared to use it in dealing with such matters as natural science. After all, it is only on the basis of a Christian philosophy, implying as it does an ultimately rational universe, that such a method can be regarded as valid. By the same token, the Christian will not adopt the attitude that he is seeking to discover something *absolutely* new, for he believes that God has already given to all things an infallible interpretation. What he is endeavoring to do is to "implicate" himself into God's creation in order that he may ascertain God's interpretation. He, therefore, carries on his scholarly activity knowing his own limitations as well as those of his techniques and, as a result, is in continual dependence upon God's help.

This statement immediately confronts us with the Christian's view of the limitations of man's techniques for acquiring knowledge. He holds that there are two aspects of this problem. Subjectively, man's intellect and emotions are those of a finite being. Consequently, he cannot grasp the significance of the whole of reality, nor can he comprehend by thought or feeling that which is beyond human experience. Some may feel that the Christian must then admit what seems to be the obverse of this: when man deals with the "phenomenal" world, he can without difficulty gain true "phenomenal" knowledge. The Christian, however, holds that even here man's knowledge is never completely trustworthy for he is a sinner whose reason and emotions are out of proper alignment. Man in his sinfulness seeks to understand and control the phenomenal without any reference whatsoever to the sovereign God. Moreover, his denial of God's universal relevancy has led to all kinds of other disorders in man himself and in his society. Consequently, man if left to himself would never be objective, scientific, or accurate. Because of his subjective disintegration resulting from sin, any scholarship would be impossible. It is only by God's gracious restraint of sin that he is able to attain any scientific results, and as in this life he never becomes perfect, even though a Christian, so his knowledge, understanding, and accuracy must be always only partial.

Added to this one limitation of man's knowledge is a second: that imposed by the infinitude of ultimate reality itself. Even if man were not a sinner and so were completely objective, rational, and accurate he could himself give no ultimate explanations of the universe. The secret things of God remain his secret (Deut. 29:29). This is one of the constant themes of biblical teaching and he who would ignore it only "darkens counsel by words without knowledge" (Job 38:2-42:6). Consequently, although man might attain by the scientific method to much knowledge of the phenomenal world, his capacity to make ultimate statements concerning that phenomenal world is definitely limited by the very nature of ultimate reality itself. When to this is added the noetic influence of sin upon man, referred to above, without God's help scholarship, as far as the Christian is concerned, would be utter folly.

But what is the Christian view of God's help in scholarly endeavor? When the Christian speaks thus, does he mean that he ignores the ordinary methods of scientific investigation in order to sit still and await some divine revelation? Some Christians may indeed hold such a position, but a self-conscious Chrisian scholar will not agree. He will use all the best proven techniques applicable to the field in which he is working, but, at the same time, he will do so deeply conscious that he is very fallible and, therefore, must be constantly vigilant lest he draw the wrong conclusions. What is more he will also pray that the Spirit of truth, the Holy Spirit, will keep him humble, objective, and accurate, realizing that only as the Spirit does so, will he, as a scholar, be able to reach valid conclusions even in the sphere of the scientifically knowable.

At this point an objection may be raised. If this is the Christian position, can the Christian scientifically defend his basic assumption of the existence of the triune God, and is he able as a Christian scholar to justify his idea of the need of help by the Holy Spirit? To this the Christian must reply that he does not intend to demonstrate these two scientifically, for despite his utmost care in employing the most accurate type of scientific measurement he is able to deal only with the phenomenal realm. Even if he were not troubled with sin and spiritual death, the scientific method still could not carry him beyond the world of human observation. And his knowledge of God is not dependent upon such techniques, for it is supra-scientific, or to use the words of Auguste Lecerf, the Christian gains this knowledge by "intellectual intuition." By this is not meant what is so commonly called '"intuition" today. God speaking in the Scriptures gives man the ultimate understanding of the universe which man recognizes to be true because his mind and understanding have been opened to receive it by the action of the Holy Spirit (I Cor. 1:18-2:16). Only as God speaks by Word and Spirit may man see beyond the phenomenal world, and therefore see even the phenomenal world itself in its true character.

To such a position the non-Christian replies, understandably enough, with an incredulous smile, "Call that scholarship?" To this the Christian has only two answers. First of all, does not the non-Christian himself begin with certain basic assumptions concerning the world and man, which on the face of them seem to be even more incredible than the Christian position? These have already been discussed. Secondly, the Christian must raise the question of results. Which position makes sense of scholarship?

When one studies the history of non-Christian scholarship, say since the days of Isaac Newton, one becomes increasingly aware of the fact that non-Christian scholarship has come to the conclusion that the universe is at bottom irrational and mysterious. Commencing his thinking with a reality which is the product of chance, as stated for instance in Sir James Jeans' *The Mysterious Universe,* it is difficult for the modern scientist not to end with ultimate irrationality. This conclusion would seem to be borne out by E. L. Mascall's Bampton Lectures for 1956, *Christian Theology and Natural Science.* But even in earlier days, before the appearance of Planck's Quantum Theory, Einstein's Theory of General Relativity, and Heisenberg's Principle of Indeterminacy which seem to point to an irrational universe, there was always a basic surd in non-Christian thinking. If the scientific method could solve all problems why did it not answer the question: What is the relation between natural law and personal freedom or responsibility? If one of these entities is accepted as ultimate, the logical conclusion is that the other is destroyed. If law is absolute, what happens to scholarship, which is supposed to be the free search for the truth by responsible human beings? If personality is absolute, what happens to law? Is it not merely a human concoction applied to experience? And if chance is ultimate, what happens to both law and personality? And where does all this leave scholarship? This would seem to be the result of the so-called "neutral scientific" approach.

But has the Christian anything better to offer? He begins with the sovereign personal Creator and Redeemer and ends with the assurance that this is a rational world; and although he cannot always comprehend its rationale, as far as he can plumb its depths he finds traces everywhere of law and order. This he holds to be the case whether one deals with the microscopic or the macroscopic in physical science, with the individual or the group in social science, with reason or intuition in the humanities. His ultimate conclusion is, therefore, that his scholarly investigations confirm his primary "intellectual intuition" of the truth of the Scriptures and their teaching. His result confirms his presupposition giving validity and value to scholarship; while the philosophical implications of the ultimate result of non-Christian scholarship, on the other hand, would seem to lead logically to scholarship's destruction.

It is only by the grace of God, therefore, that the non-Christian is preserved from total scepticism. He assumes, albeit unconsciously and frequently in opposition to his conscious theoretical presuppositions, that this is a rational, orderly, and understandable world. But this he can do logically only on Christian assumptions. For this reason the Christian holds very firmly that "a true scientific procedure is impossible unless we hold to the presupposition of God."[1] Although the Christian and the non-Christian scholars are far apart at the starting point, the non-Christian is obliged to shift his superstructure on to the Christian foundation or admit that all is chaos. The Christian on the other hand, holding to his original position, believes that it is Christianity which not only alone makes scholarship possible, but in doing so also demonstrates the truth of the Gospel of Jesus Christ.

The Christian Attitude to Non-Christian Scholarship

What has been said, however, immediately raises the question of the proper Christian attitude to the results of non-Christian scholarship. If a piece of scholarly research and writing has been produced by an unbeliever, should one, because of its non-Christian authorship, condemn it as unsound? Perhaps to some Christians this would seem to be the best approach. After all, have not the non-Christian scholars of various types produced some theories such as evolution, economic determinism, communism, and the like? That is true; but perhaps a

[1] C. Van Til, *Christian-Theistic Evidences*, p. ii.

more thorough study of the origins of those ideas which Christians often condemn might indicate that they have arisen primarily because Christians did not attempt to provide a Christian interpretation for the problems or phenomena with which they deal. Moreover, it may even appear that in these concepts some elements are by no means erroneous. Therefore, it will be useful to make an examination at this point of what the Christian view of non-Christian scholarship should be.

Probably two of the best examples of what should be the Christian's attitude toward non-Christian scholarship are found in the histories of Moses and Daniel, both of whom were trained in all the lore and wisdom of what today would be called unbelieving science. The Apostle Paul was a man with the same type of background, and there are no doubt others to whom we could point, including Isaiah, Nehemiah, and Luke. They all apparently made use of the training, the knowledge, and the understanding which they had received from completely unbelieving teachers.

It would seem that God in his dealings with man enables even the unbelieving scholar to learn much and understand much of this universe. By what has come to be called "Common Grace," he preserves the non-Christian from the absolute error and folly to which his denial of divine sovereignty should logically lead. Thus men have made great and marvelous discoveries concerning nature, history, and society. They have produced wonderful works of art, music, and engineering. They have even evolved very impressive systems of philosophy in attempting to reason concerning the ultimate meaning of things. And all these the Christian must recognize and use if he is to achieve anything in the field of scholarship.

Yet the Christian must always be on his guard. The non-Christian, despite his professed adherence to "the facts" alone, is no more objective than the Christian. He begins his reasoning with assumptions and very often uses his research to prove a point upon which he has already decided before the beginning of his investigation. Moreover, the non-Christian scholar is as prone as any individual to use the results of his work for his own enrichment, exaltation, or self-satisfaction. The result is that much scholarly work is a mixture of both fact and fiction. Thus the Christian must always be critical, never taking any scholarly theory too seriously nor as the final word even of the scholar who propounds it, for in the light of further knowledge the theory may seem to be wrong, one-sided, or much more limited in scope than originally recognized. Therefore, no scholarly hypothesis is to be either accepted as a sure proof of Christianity or feared as the destroyer of the faith. All scholarly work must be criticized, for it is but the work of fallible, finite, and fallen men.

If the Christian scholar keeps this in mind he will not fall into the error of accepting every new interpretation which arises. Man always seeks for unity in his experience, with the result that he continually looks for a single cause or explanation for all things. During the past century and a half every field of scholarly endeavor has experienced the rise and decline of explanations which attempt to interpret all temporal phenomena in terms of a single force: natural selection, Malthusianism, economic determinism, and many others. To the Christian many of these have merit in that they bring out certain neglected aspects of reality. But ultimately:

> God moves in a mysterious way
> His wonders to perform;
> He plants His footsteps in the sea,
> And rides upon the storm.

Therefore, the Christian must always look upon any theory of a single form of causation with suspicion and examine it very carefully before he considers accepting it as an adequate interpretation for all phenomena even in a limited field. He must continually be skeptical of all such hypotheses.

Going even farther, one's criticism of the non-Christian's work must point out its structural weaknesses which result from an unbelieving approach. It should be made clear that even those who claim to start merely with the facts "and follow them whithersoever they lead" are in truth beginning with a whole universe of assumptions. Moreover, one must also recognize that often these assumptions and the conclusions derived from them are inconsistent, as when one begins by postulating an ordered world and concludes that reality is ultimately chance, or vice versa. The Christian, while acknowledging the achievements of human scholarship in the immediate field of "the phenomenal," must continually point out that if it does not begin and end with a sovereign God, it is fundamentally self-contradictory and that its basic assumption of the self-existence of finite reality, if carried out to its logical conclusion, cannot but lead to the destruction of all scholarship.

The Christian Attitude to Christian Scholarship

In the light of his somewhat negative view of non-Christian scholarship, it seems only right that the Christian should state what he believes to be the nature of true scholarship and, above all other things, practice it. At this point, however, despite all that has been said, not a few devout Christians may still ask: Why bother about scholarship at all? To this there are many answers, of which only a few can be presented here.

In the first place, Christian scholarship is required because it is necessary to understand Christianity, and that is not possible by an *uninformed* intuition or sentiment. Another reason is that it is necessary in order to defend Christianity. Some people, it is true, feel that a scholarly apologetic for the faith is impossible or unnecesssary. But if we believe that Christianity reveals the ultimate meaning of all that is, surely there must be a very important place for a scholarly exposition and defense of its teachings. Quite as important is the fact that scholarly research is needed for an application of Christianity in every field of human action and thought. Mere Pietism or sanctimonious talk of Christianity being "the answer to the world's problems" amounts to very little unless Christians can apply it effectively in all spheres of human life.

Such scholarship is not anti-spiritual, for the Christian must carry out his scholarly work in complete dependence on the Holy Spirit, since he alone is the guide to all truth (John 16:13). Moreover, the Christian scholar must realize that all his abilities, capacities, and strength are the gifts of the Spirit. If he does his scholarly research and thinking in the light of these fundamental presuppositions, he will realize that he is not doing them merely for his own increase of knowledge, but to gain a greater understanding of the creative, providential, and redemptive work of God that he may more fully show forth the divine glory. If these be the dynamic and objective of Christian scholarship, how can it be unspiritual?

Now some Christians will agree to what has been said thus far, but in reality they are thinking of these comments as applying only to theological and biblical studies. They will agree that we must have Christian scholarship in the fields of the Old and New Testaments, systematic and practical theology, and even in church history. But at the margins of these disciplines they would stop. While they may not say so in so many words, Christianity in their thinking has nothing to do with physics, chemistry, biology, economics, literature, music, or art. The best thing for the Christian to do is to leave such matters to the non-Christian who has nothing better to do with his time!

But if the Christian truly believes that behind the physical reality of the universe there is one who is the Creator, Sustainer, and Governor of all things; moreover, if he believes that this same Being is the redeemer of rebellious men through Jesus Christ, how can he hold such ideas? All things, all fields of knowledge, are there for the Christian's investigation and he ignores them at his own peril. This is the continual theme of many of the older Protestant writers. Jerome Zanche, for instance, in his *De Operibus Dei* points out that theology is not to be separated from physics, for which the Bible sets forth the basic philosophy of the natural sciences. Physics itself is the demonstration of the physical causes, principles, and effects of things and men. He therefore urged theologians to study the physical sciences since in them God shows forth his great power, wisdom, and goodness, by which he brings man into fuller knowledge of himself.[2]

If modern Christians are prepared to accept such a position, it would seem logical that they should enter into all fields of scholarship. But if they do so, they must meet the two fundamental requirments. The first is that they must know their own position as Christians. This means that they should be well-grounded theologically and philosophically in the faith, in order to keep a continual check on their own and others' work. Just as important as this, however, is the necessity of their being well-grounded in their own particular fields of study. No one can be a scholar of any type, Christian or not, if he does not submit himself to the discipline of his own specialty. Nor should the Christian ever feel that it is possible to solve the problems of the universe by a few "general Christian propositions" or a few well-chosen biblical texts. If any scholar is to understand the forces and patterns of nature and history he must

---

[2] *De Operibus Dei Intra Spacium Sex Dierum Creatis,* Hanover, 1597, 2nd ed., p. 289.

pry the answers loose with every tool at his disposal. Only then will he be able to give a true interpretation of the immediate and proximate facts of the universe.

At the same time, Christians must be extremely careful if they attempt to link their understanding of their *immediate* "environment" with their interpretation of the *ultimate* meaning of the universe, *i.e.*, with God's being, purpose, and action. For one thing, as those who are still sinful human beings, Christians must realize that there is always the possibility and indeed the probability of error in their interpretation of the Scriptures. Luther's rejection of Copernicus' heliocentric model of the universe on supposedly scriptural grounds is a warning to be extremely careful lest we misinterpret and misuse the Bible. There is, however, another reason for careful walking with regard to this matter. The Christian's ultimate explanation of all things is the "Eternal," but the mundane facts with which he is dealing are temporal. To link the two together, to produce a valid nexus between them requires more knowledge and understanding than the capabilities of finite humanity seem to warrant. For example, it would be exceedingly dangerous for a Christian historian to attempt to demonstrate why God brought about the defeat of Hitler. Mixing time and eternity is not the work of any scholar!

Keeping this in mind, the Christian physicist will avoid the error of attempting to prove Christian doctrine from natural phenomena, and the Christian historian will be very careful not to attempt to demonstrate the work of the Holy Spirit in history from historical facts. On the other hand, under the control of their Christian faith and in the belief that the truth concerning nature and history is to a certain extent discoverable by man, Christians will do their utmost to grasp the meaning of the world in which God has placed them, knowing that by so doing they are indeed glorifying him.

If the Christian scholar follows this course, he will undoubtedly make it plain that Christianity and scholarship are by no means incompatible. And if there are enough Christians who are prepared to devote themselves to scholarship, it will not be long before the opinion which is so prevalent today that Christianity and scholarship are in conflict will begin to disappear. Men will once again begin to realize that true scholarship and true Christianity are indeed eminently compatible, with the result that there may gradually develop in scholarly circles a climate of opinion far more favorable to Christianity than exists at the present time. The obscurantism of so many Christians on matters not directly connected with their faith, tends to prejudice thinking people against the Gospel. Christians should by their scholarly pursuits show that their faith is not in conflict with that scholarship which does not extrapolate itself beyond legitimate limits, but attempts to keep within its God-given bounds.

Scholarship The Gift Of God

From what has been said above, it should be clear that scholarship is not something which the Christian should condemn, but rather something in which he should rejoice. After all, it is man's duty to understand the reality which God has created, sustains, and redeems. Though the unbeliever does not recognize that this is what he is actually doing, nevertheless he is contributing to precisely this objective. He may use the results of his studies to attack the idea of the very existence of God, but in so doing he really assumes that there is a valid interpretation of the universe, which, he must admit, he himself could never formulate on the basis of his own, and even of all human, experience. Consequently, he is dragging in quite unconsciously and unwillingly an idea which requires the sovereign God. Indeed the God he ejected from the front door he must now smuggle in by the rear.

Thus albeit unconsciously, the atheist, as Calvin maintains, by his very apodictical denial of God, shows that he must assume the sovereign God's existence. Scholarship, therefore, is not something for the Christian to despise, but rather for him to recognize as perhaps the summit of all man's achievement under the sun.

Yet he must never be carried away by the accomplishments of the scholar as though the scholar were a law unto himself. His chief end in life is to think God's thoughts after him, God's thoughts revealed in the Scriptures, in creation, and in history. And whatever he accomplishes in this endeavor he does by the grace of God alone, working through the agency of the Holy Spirit, who leads to all truth. Therefore, the Christian must ultimately give God the glory for the achievements and discoveries of scholarship, knowing that in him, by him, and to him are all things, world without end.

When this point of view is adopted by Christians, much of the fear of scholarship will depart. They will see that scholarship, rightly understood, with its limitations properly appreciated, is not something which will destroy the faith, but rather which will lead on to a greater understanding of the divine power and wisdom. Those who keep this in mind will come to recognize scholarship, and particularly Christian scholarship, as a God-given means of knowing and glorifying him who is the Lord of all things, Creator, Sustainer, and Redeemer.

CHAPTER II

THE CHRISTIAN AND THE SCIENTIFIC METHOD

The Present Christian Attitude to the Scientific Method

Since the beginning of the seventeenth century man's confidence and admiration for scientific activity has steadily grown until today he has become dependent in almost every aspect of life upon the results of scientific research. Whether he has liked it or not science has by virtue of its advances come increasingly to dominate his thought-patterns as indicated by the more common use of scientific terms in ordinary conversation. Western man has reached the position where he believes that practically every aspect of experience, including one's religious beliefs, may be analyzed properly only if one employs the methods of natural science.[1] For this reason the Christian has during the past century or more felt himself torn between two attitudes to science, and this ambivalence has caused him much uncertainty in his attitude toward the scientific method itself.

The Christian cannot, and indeed should not, deny the accomplishments of scientists, nor the effectiveness of the scientific method. After all, whether he recognizes the fact or not, both his necessities and his luxuries have come to him largely as a result of scientific endeavor. The car he drives, the airplane in which he travels, the food that he eats and the clothes that he wears to a large extent owe their existence to the scientific research of the past century. Moreover, many of the contemporary social phenomena and patterns trace their origin back to the same source. Consequently, he may never fail to acknowledge that the use of the scientific method has

[1] E. F. Caldin, *The Power and Limits of Science*, London, 1949, p. 3.

aided greatly in the opening up of human culture in this world.[2]

On the other hand, the Christian often feels that he has abundant cause to fear the development which has taken place through the use of the scientific method. For one thing, one cannot always be sure that the so-called advances in science which seem at first to introduce an amelioration of man's condition, have always truly helped man. This is particularly striking when one realizes that only too frequently unbelievers have attempted to employ the scientific method as a weapon against the Christian gospel itself. Adopting a fundamentally naturalistic point of view, many scientists have rejected any idea of man as more than a fortuitous extension of the animal kingdom, a denial of the Christian doctrines of creation, fall and redemption in Jesus Christ. To this Christians have usually reacted with disfavor and fear. The scientific method they feel is godless and atheistic, and as far as possible no Christian should have anything to do with it.

In the light of our present dependence on science, such an adverse attitude can hardly come to expression in practice. Therefore, a good many Christians accept the results of scientific research, as applied to everyday living, but desire to stay as far from it as possible whenever it deals with the theoretical even though it is limited strictly to its own particular sphere. This often leads the Christian to impose upon his thinking a division. He regards the scientific investigation of the material world as something apart from his Christian faith. The study of physics, chemistry, history, sociology and other spheres of experience, he looks upon as really autonomous so that scientific research has nothing to do with, or to say about, his Christian faith, and the Christian

[2] One might add that a good many Christians fear science because it upsets their basically Aristotelian interpretation of the Bible's statements. *Cf.* H. Dooyeweerd, *A New Critique of Theoretical Thought*, Philadelphia, 1953, I, 510.

faith reciprocates by having nothing to say, except in most general terms, about science and scientific research. Thus the Christian, particularly if he is a scientist, often develops a two-compartment mind devoted respectively to scientific investigation and to the Christian faith.

Such a point of view has little to recommend it, for it implies, if it does not actually maintain, that God's sovereignty and Christ's redemptive work apply only to man's religious experience, leaving all other aspects of man's experience and activity to the domination of a virtual naturalism. One can hardly call this a Christian solution to the problem. To deal with it, therefore, Christians in this third quarter of the twentieth century must take a very close look at modern science and in particular at the scientific method. They must endeavor to see it as it really is, and they must also attempt to understand what it involves, not merely in its practical application, but in its theoretical implications for them as Christians.

When they have made up their minds about this, they should then set forth the Christian view concerning the scientific method, its presuppositions, its validity and its scope. Only then will they make some impact upon scientific thought in a critical but positive manner. Their interpretation, to be sure, should not take the form of a merely edifying confession of faith which may help one to appreciate the gospel more fully, but which leaves the problem of scientific investigation untouched. Rather they should try to permeate scientific studies with the Christian concept of truth, in order that they may make manifest that only when built on a Christian foundation can scientific research be more than the technical study of phenomena.[3]

[3] *Ibid.*, II, 572.

To study anything, one should first of all have some idea of what one plans to investigate. For this reason we must begin by asking ourselves what we mean by the "scientific method." To answer this question a considerable number of books have recently appeared on the market, but they all seem to come to one particular point. The scientific method is a method of asking questions of the temporal, phenomenal world whereby the scientist hopes to obtain answers which will provide him with the means of describing the "regularities underlying diverse events."[4] Many techniques of investigation have their places in this general method both in terms of instruments employed and the use of the instruments. Martin Deutsch has subsumed the various methods under observation, testing and measurement.[5] When one has obtained certain results from investigation one then goes on to construct models and formulate laws which actually surpass immediate observations. These laws in turn, in the hands of a great scientist, may become general concepts, hypotheses on a grand scale, opening up new spheres of study.[6]

But what determines the method which one uses? What guides the investigator in the techniques which he employs? Usually the question he desires to have answered. The scientist directs his query to nature in a particular way in order that the answer will contain a minimum amount of variables and irrelevancies.[7] As Dooyeweerd has pointed out: "Experiments are always pointed to the solution of theoretical questions which the scientist himself has raised and formulated."[8] And these

---

[4] D. Lerner, *Evidence and Inference*, Glencoe, Ill., 1959, p. 13.

[5] *Ibid.*, pp. 102 f.

[6] Caldin, *op. cit.*, pp. 53 f.; J. B. Conant, *Modern Science and Modern Man*, New York, 1953, pp. 47 f.

[7] Caldin, *op. cit.*, p. 18.

[8] *Op. cit.*, I, 561; W. Heisenberg, *Physics and Philosophy*, London, 1959, p. 38.

questions usually receive their form from the laws of the sphere of temporal reality which the scientist is investigating, modified by the state of knowledge of that sphere at the particular time, and limited by the competence of the investigator himself. Thus even the questions posed involve more than a mechanical type of inquiry.

Behind both the scientist's question and his understanding and interpretation of the answer he receives lie certain basic assumptions about himself and about the temporal reality which he seeks to open up. When working in a limited field of research this does not easily become apparent, for many scientists with no philosophical interest take most of their basic principles as axiomatic and relate them merely to technical problems. But when one attempts to carry one's thinking out into wider spheres, applying one's results to reality on a grand scale, one immediately becomes conscious of many philosophical and even religious assumptions. Thus the questions which one poses in the search for truth involve one's whole basic outlook on God and man.

Before turning to an examination of the metaphysical religious presuppositions behind the modern scientific method, however, in order to understand what one means by the term "scientific method," one should attempt to see how it has developed over the past five or six centuries. It did not spring full armed, like Athena, from the head of a Galileo, a Bacon or even a Newton. It has developed gradually and slowly, piling up precept upon precept, here a little, there a little, and even today, despite the views of many, it has not reached final completion and probably never will. Consequently if one desires to understand the scientific method one must look back over its history in order to gain a proper perspective on it as it is today.

Going back to the Middle Ages one finds that an attitude existed then very different from the modern outlook. The medieval thinker, his mind dominated by Platonic and Aristotelian concepts, thought of reality as made up of two realms: nature and grace. While the realm of grace was that of the church, of revelation, of heaven, the realm of nature was that of the world in which he lived here and now, in which man's mind possessed relative autonomy. In fact if he used his reason carefully he could reason independently to the borders of grace, proving the existence of God, of right and wrong and many other truths.[9] He would do this by seeking to discover, by the use of reason, the true essences of things, e. g., the dogginess in which all dogs participate. In this way the philosopher could gain an understanding of the nature of these essences. Then building them up into their proper hierarchy of being until he reached the limit of nature, he would come to know the world as it truly is. Although his passions might lead him astray in this endeavor these he might overcome by the infusion of God's grace.

Behind this "scientific" attitude lies an interpretation both of the universe and of man's place in it. The physical temporal universe lies open to human rational analysis, so that man by reasoning correctly, accurately and effectively can gain a proper understanding of it without taking God into account. Thus man needs only the restraint of his passions in order that he may gain true knowledge of the world in which he lives. Both he and the temporal cosmos possess autonomy in their own right, and only when he attempts to step beyond the temporal cosmos must he really look to God for knowledge and understanding. Thus grace builds upon an already independent and autonomous nature.[10]

In the fourteenth century the medieval concept of the relation of nature and grace began to change. It now

---

[9] H. Dooyeweerd, *In the Twilight of Western Thought*, Philadelphia, 1960, p. 44.

[10] Thomas Aquinas, *Summa Contra Gentiles*, bk. I, chaps. III ff.

became a matter of nature against grace. Religious truth might well contradict the natural truth discovered and accepted by man's reason. Moreover, men began to lose interest in seeking for essences, concentrating upon the individual phenomenon experienced. After all, one sees in nature only individual items. The nominalists said very bluntly that the so-called universals or essences had no reality, but simply represented names which men had devised. To seek for universals led nowhere. Men should investigate the individual. Although some natural philosophers such as Roger Bacon, influenced by Augustine of Hippo, continued to insist that individual phenomena depended for their being and nature upon the divinely ordained, uniform laws of the universe, others such as William of Occam held to the more atomistic interpretations.[11]

The ultimate objectives of the new way of thinking became clear in the Renaissance when men increasingly regarded the realm of grace as irrelevant and laid all their stress upon man in this world. Regarding man as a microcosm, a universe in miniature, they thought of him as a being who by his own will-power and efforts could elevate himself almost to the divine, and yet at the same time remain part of the cosmos in which he lived, subject to the rule of nature.[12] The realm of grace, if it existed, man did not need. Fortune ruled all so that man had to try by his reason to overcome her vagaries whether good or ill. Renaissance thinkers stressed man and his abilities, but conveniently ignored the laws of nature which guided and directed both him and his cosmic environment.

By 1500, therefore, scientific method appeared in many guises. The true-blue Aristotelian, dependent on "the philosopher's" authority, usually followed a fully deduc-

[11] Dooyeweerd, *Twilight*, p. 44; A. C. Crombie, *Augustine to Galileo*, London, 1957, pp. 212 ff.

[12] Good examples of this point of view are Machiavelli, Pico della Mirandola and Castiglione.

tive method. The convinced and consistent nominalist, on the other hand, stressed the study and classification of the individual phenomenon. A third element consisted of the practical scientists who, to make sense of the physical universe, found themselves obliged to assume a certain amount of uniformitarianism in nature, in order that they might make some generalizations concerning individual phenomena. And yet even this last concept of nature had within it many traits of the older thinking, for only too often the natural laws themselves semed to be subject to the influences of occult forces such as those exercised by the planets or demons. Uncertainty characterized much of the thinking of the time.

Into this somewhat chaotic state of scientific thought the Protestant Reformation, and, in particular, Calvin, introduced a note of stability. With his emphasis upon the doctrines of creation, providence and redemption, he turned men's minds in the direction of a solid law-basis for the universe which man by virtue of his creation in God's image and his redemption by God's grace could truly, although in a limited way, understand.[13] In Calvin's thought all the particulars which man experiences in this world are bound together and subject to God's created laws, which alone make it possible to talk of a cosmos rather than a chaos. Moreover, through this cosmos God offers a natural revelation of himself that man should see the divine origin of all things.[14] Thus in Protestant circles natural physical law became a fundamental presupposition of all scientific thought. In a certain sense this brought about a restoration of the medieval "law-idea," only it had now lost its autonomy by virtue of the Calvinistic doctrines of creation and providence.

Although the Reformation helped to counteract the atomism of Renaissance humanism, the Calvinistic con-

[13] Dooyeweerd, *New Critique*, I, 510 f.

[14] John Calvin, *Institutes of the Christian Religion*, I, xiv, 20 f.; I, xvi, 4. Cf Chapt. III *infra*.

cept of law soon suffered secularization. The humanist, stressing the necessity of man's domination of nature, reduced the Christian concept of "replenishing and ruling over" the physical world to a natural law, which lost its grounding in the sovereignty of God to become something independent and self-existent. Both the individual phenomenon and the law became abstractions, for the phenomenon existed in complete isolation while the law had no concrete content. The only difficulty was that one could not analyze pure abstractions or come to know them except perhaps by mathematics or geometry. Thus the essence of scientific investigation became the observation and measurement of the *functions* of particulars, leading eventually to the discovery and elaboration of laws.[15]

Although the concept of law in nature had by no means completely disappeared from natural philosphy during the Renaissance, the philosphers themselves never seem to have incorporated it fully into their methodology until the end of the sixteenth century. Copernicus, the Polish ecclesiastic, had in his *De Revolutionibus Orbium Coelestium* touched upon law and its relation to scientific method, but not until the appearance of Galileo Galilei, Francis Bacon and René Descartes did the scientist attempt a systematic exposition of the new ways to study nature.[16] Galileo worked out practical problems at first by rule of thumb and from his results deduced certain laws of motion. Bacon and Descartes carried the matter further. Believing that God had created and sustains all things, Bacon held that man must seek the "form" of the phenomena by which he meant the necessary and sufficient condition of its existence, i. e., the laws by which it exists.[17] To achieve this, Bacon held, one should frame hypotheses which one might then test by experience, and if corroborated, the hypotheses would

[15] Crombie, *op. cit.*, pp. 308 ff.

[16] *Ibid.*

[17] W. C. Kneale, "Scientific Method" in *Encyclopedia Britannica*, 1957, XX.

become general principles. René Descartes added an additional element by insisting that self-consciousness and geometrical order formed the foundation of all knowledge of the universe. He wished to break down all experience in order that he might rebuild it geometrically.[18] These early formulations of scientific methods had as their successors men such as Kepler, Harvey, Huygens, Boyle, and above all others, Sir Isaac Newton, whose great work *Philosophiae Naturalis Principia Mathematica* (1687) showed quite clearly the nature of this concept of scientific knowledge.[19]

To Newton and his contemporaries natural philosophy had nothing to do with ultimates. Although Newton himself made his name primarily as a scientist, and much of his interest lay in the realm of theology, he never brought the two together. He adopted the position that the phenomenal world to all intents and purposes is an autonomous world. To understand it one does not merely concentrate upon individual phenomena, but must attempt to subsume all under general categories of natural law. To do so the scientist must equate the function of the phenomenon with its nature, and physical reality becomes nothing more ultimate than this law. Moreover, since this is the character of the universe, men, by analogy, accepted the method employed by Newton to study the movements of the heavenly bodies, as the only method by which one could know anything.[20]

The eighteenth century one might well call the century of Newton. His disciples carried his views and techniques into every possible sphere of study, and as they did so one notices that the idea of even an absentee-god begins to fade away. Newton might say that he did not deal with absolutes, many of his followers did not possess

---

[18] Dooyeweerd, *Twilight*, p. 49; H. Butterfield, *The Origins of Modern Science*, London, 1950, pp. 83 ff.

[19] *Ibid.*, pp. 65 ff.; Dooyeweerd, *New Critique*, I, pp. 553 ff.

[20] Dooyeweerd, *Twilight*, p. 50; Bavinck, *The Philosophy of Revelation*, New York, 1909, p. 67.

such modesty. They, rather, began to pride themselves on the fact that no absolute existed beyond their scientific measurements, so that by the end of the century God had become to Laplace an unneeded hypothesis. Yet this declaration of independence did not answer all their questions. With a world governed by absolute natural law what happened to human freedom? Could one believe that man possessed any real freedom? What value did his thought have, if it did no more than simply register the impressions of sense experiences under the control of natural law? If, on the other hand, man was truly free, what then happened to natural law, at least as far as it affected man? One could not have it both ways.

Unfortunately for Western thought, the eighteenth century Evangelical Revival had little to say to the contemporary scientific world. With the exception of George Whitefield and of a few men in Scotland and Holland, the main stream of the movement flowed in the Arminian channel. These evangelicals laid their great stress upon man, his abilities and his independence over against God, so that the Arminian Wesley could declare to the Calvinist Whitefield, "Your God is my devil." Consequently, any attempt by the evangelicals at a Christian interpretation of the place of the individual human ego within a world of law never gained much currency. Calling upon men to place their faith in Christ, they never really sought to apply their Christianity more widely.

Immanuel Kant, who came out of a pietistic background, sought on purely rational grounds to solve the problem of scientific knowledge, of natural law and human personality, by separating the mechanical, mathematical universe from that of human freedom. Man's decisions he placed in the moral sphere, while he held that mathematical and mechanical scientific knowledge came by man's subsuming the chaos of experience under the logical categories of his own understanding. The scientist knew the world scientifically when he subjected it to the rational laws of his own mind. The only difficulty was that man himself forms part of the chaotic, mechanical universe, which would seem to indicate that scientific knowledge has thus become something which really does not represent the world of experience at all. For this reason any truly logical or empirical analysis of the facts would seem to be impossible.

From the days of Kant, partially as a result of his thought and partially as an outgrowth of Hegel's stress upon history as the process of the *Weltgeist* coming to self-consciousness, men sought to solve the problem of scientific knowledge by two means. The first, derived from the writings of Auguste Comte, was known as positivism. The scientist simply took the facts as they presented themselves in his experience, i.e., experimentally, and from these measured facts, by means of hypotheses, formulated laws. Philosophy had nothing to do with the case, for metaphysics belonged to an earlier and less enlightened phase of human development.[21] Alongside the positivist stood the historicist who held that in the biological and social aspects of experience one needed to know historical development. Since the world of animal and man had evolved over aeons of time, to know and understand the present situation, one must know the past. Function and measurement thus received the addition of the idea of development which the historicist hoped would help explain, and perhaps correlate, the idea of law with that of personal freedom. By this means man could finally reach the truth.

In the sciences of physics and chemistry the result of seventeenth- and eighteenth-century research was uniformitarianism. Newton had held that laws which ruled here on earth explained certain phenomena, so if one observed similar reactions in the heavens, they obviously

---

[21] Dooyeweerd, *New Critique*, I, 546 ff; *The Positive Philosophy of Auguste Comte*, H. Martineau, tr., London, 1853, I, 1-3.

ruled also in the celestial area. After a certain struggle, uniformitarianism in biology, geology and paleontology gave way to an evolutionary interpretation, although even here a type of uniformitarianism in the historical process continued to dominate. Processes observable today in nature must have ruled nature from the beginning.[22] The development in these fields inevitably helped to produce "the social sciences" which attempted to provide a measured, functional and developmental explanation of economics, political science, religion and even of history itself. Thus by the end of the third quarter of the nineteenth century, most scientists had become quite confident that they would eventually obtain an explanation of all the facts of experience.

The ground for this confidence lay in their faith in the so-called "scientific method." All the scientists of the latter part of the nineteenth century insisted that to obtain adequate scientific results one had to approach one's researches with no preconceptions and without reference to any authority. After preliminary observation of the phenomena under study the scientist should frame an hypothesis, which usually involved the construction, perhaps only in the mind, of a mechanical model. Then followed a series of experiments to test the hypothesis, which, depending on the empirical results, might need appropriate alteration or modification. Once the investigator had verified his hypothesis, he next proceeded to interpret it in terms of unifying theories which he usually called laws and to extend it to unobserved cases.[23] The crux of this whole technique lay in the formulation of hypotheses and the construction of mechanical models, but the scientist offered no explanation to account for the possibility of hypotheses posses-

---

[22] R. Hooykaas, *Natural Law and Divine Miracle*, Leiden, 1960, describes the manner in which the concepts regarding science developed during the nineteenth century.

[23] Caldin, *op. cit.*, pp. 21, 52 ff.; Conant, *op. cit.*, pp. 55 ff.; Kneale, *op. cit.*

sing validity in a purely mechanical universe. Such was the situation about 1890.

By the opening of World War I, because of the work of Morley and Michelson on light, of the Curies on radium, and of various scientists in other fields, supported by the mathematical studies of men such as Einstein, except in limited and practical areas the nineteenth-century concepts faced rejection. As men delved deeper into the nature of the atom or of the celestial universe, they found that many of the old accepted laws simply did not stand up to empirical investigation. As Planck studied the characteristics of light he found himself forced to formulate the quantum theory which he had to combine with a wave theory, two hypotheses which seemed mutually contradictory, but both of which met certain empirical tests. Heisenberg then propounded the view that one could never determine the true position or velocity of an electron, for in attempting to locate such a small entity one affected both position and velocity. Thus to man the universe is in the final analysis a mystery, the image frequently formed by the scientist being "the symbolic anthropomorphic representation of the basically inconceivable atomic process."[24]

What does this mean for the scientific outlook and for the scientific method? The scientist now tends to reject the old ideas of attaining scientific understanding by "cook-book methods."[25] He tries new models which no longer follow the old mechanical pattern but tend to become mathematical equations or statistical studies, and necessarily so, because no sense organs can make direct observations of the sub-atomic phenomena. In so creating his model, however, the scientist finds it necessary to disregard certain aspects or effects of the actions of the phenomena as irrelevant because they do not fit in with

---

[24] Deutsch in Lerner, *op. cit.*, p. 96; Conant, *op. cit.*, pp. 48 ff., 66 ff.

[25] *Ibid.*, pp. 41 ff.

the preconceived structure. He does this simply on the basis of his intuition.[26] As P. W. Bridgeman has pointed out, the scientist is now reaching the boundaries of scientific knowledge, but boundaries established not so much by the construction of the world, as by the limitations of his own perceptions and comprehension.[27] This is a far cry from the self-assurance of the eighteenth century.

As one might well expect, such views have forced a major re-orientation in the concepts of scientific method. While the old techniques still produce results in the applied science of a company laboratory, scientists no longer regard them as providing the answers to the ultimate riddles of the universe. They now tend to think in terms of great general concepts, hypotheses on a grand scale. As one reads various writers on the subject one comes repeatedly across the words "imagination," "rational," "intuition," "stimulation to further investigation."[28] Conant has declared flatly that no longer may the scientist think of himself as mapping out the universe like a geographer. Scientific theories, he must regard merely as "guides to human action," and perhaps as "an extension of common sense."[29] Others, however, such as Sir James Jeans, go further and believe that while empirical investigation is still necessary, ultimately the universe in which we live is a universe of chance. If one accepts such views, however, it would seem that one casts doubt on any scientific investigation, and even on the scientific method itself.[30]

---

[26] *Ibid.*, pp. 75 f.; Lerner, *op. cit.*, 96 ff.

[27] Conant, *op. cit.*, p. 87.

[28] *Ibid.*, p. 47; Caldin, *op. cit.*, pp. 22 f.; A. D. Ritchie, *Studies in the History and Methods of the Sciences*, Edinburgh, 1958, pp. 80 f.

[29] Conant, *op. cit.*, p. 101.

[30] Sir James Jeans, *The Mysterious Universe*, New York, Cambridge, 1944, chap. I.

The Philosophical Presuppositions of the Scientific Method

Ever since the sixteenth-century, scientists have more often than not maintained that they do not bother with matters of philosophy or religion. Their aim is to find out the truth about the cosmos, and to this end their only true interest lies in accurate measurement of, and exact comprehension of, the functions of temporal phenomena. Since they seek primarily to develop techniques for the observation and measurement of phenomena, they require no presuppositions.[31] As one can see from what has been said above, this position has begun to lose some of its acceptance in the twentieth-century world. When speaking of "general concepts," or of "hypotheses on a grand scale," modern scientists, or at least some of them, have found it necessary to recognize that they actually do set forth cosmologies, interpretations of the temporal cosmos, which involve the whole of reality itself. They may no longer confine their investigations to matters of technique, but despite themselves have become philosophers, with presumptions concerning both themselves and nature. Consequently, it should not present as much difficulty today as it used to in the past to prove that scientists, for all their professed objectivity, have behind their views of the universe, and so behind their method of investigation, a philosophy which they should recognize.

If one commences by examining the scientist's presuppositions concerning his field of study, frequently one discovers that he adopts the attitude that he may analyse his sphere of interest without reference to any others. Chemists and physicists have found themselves forced to forsake such an attitude on many occasions, particularly in atomic research. On the other hand, a good many scientists working in their laboratories forget

[31] Dooyeweerd, *Critique*, I, 550 f.

about the other sciences, and even deny the relevance of social and philosophical studies. The tendency is to forget their work's relationship to reality as a whole. One may hardly experience surprise, therefore, when they deny the existence of any vertical relationship as exemplified by religious faith.[32]

Another assumption of the scientist which one frequently encounters is that the scientific method deals with natural-reality-in-itself. While the scientist may not find it possible to analyze atomic phenomena in an exact manner so that he can identify and plot the course of an individual atom, nevertheless when he measures and analyzes the functions of a natural object he comes to know it. He usually does not consider it necessary to relate his results to other fields, nor to a basic and fundamental philosophical view of reality as a whole. He feels that he operates above and beyond such necessity or limitation. By this scientific means he has come to know the object at least as far as it is knowable to man.[33]

This involves a further presupposition: that all phenomena exist under the laws of the field or sphere which they operate. E. F. Caldin has pointed out, for instance, that since physics deals with inanimate matter, the physicist seeks for laws of general behavior of the phenomena under investigation, laws which one may know by means of measurement and express in mathematical equations. The results so obtained he then applies even to unobserved phenomena. This means, of course, that the scientist by analogy declares that the universe possesses a basic order and law-structure which extends outside his own field of investigation. Even Heisenberg's principle of indeterminacy does not mean that no law exists or that causality is a figment of the imagination. It merely says that man cannot discover them in sub-atomic matter by empirical means. To make

---

[32] Dooyeweerd, *op. cit.*, II, 577; *Twilight*, pp. 8 f.
[33] Caldin, *op. cit.*, pp. 26, 38 ff.; Lerner, *op. cit.*, p. 12.

such a statement, however, involves belief in the orderliness of nature. Thus in spite of the scepticism of a Hume or a Bertrand Russell, a scientist in order to carry out his investigations must make certain basic assumptions concerning law and order in the universe. Even Sir James Jeans' mysterious universe seems to require a mathematical framework in which to operate.[34]

Does the modern scientist believe that by the scientific method he has reached ultimate reality? To this the answer would seem to be, No. He holds much the position of Newton who said that he did not deal with ultimate matters. He may state his hypotheses on a grand scale, develop his general concepts as "generally" as he will, but in the end, as most leading scientific thinkers today admit, he has not really advanced beyond the physical world. Scientifically, mystery or chance lie just across the border line of all that he may know, and not infrequently the scientist desires to leave it there, claiming that he neither knows, nor wishes to know anything beyond the physical law-structure or measurements of the universe.[35]

Yet all along, in his believing that the physical cosmos operates according to law or has dimensions susceptible of measurement, that it is knowable through empirical investigation, and that it consists of certain basic elements such as energy, he has in reality made much wider assumptions concerning the temporal universe than he admits. He may end by talking about mystery or chance, but his fundamental Kantianism cannot stand up to the basic questions of whence the laws, whence the energy, or what is the assurance of the truth of analogies? Can these arise by chance from chaos?

---

[34] *Ibid.*, pp. 9, 15 ff., 25, 46 f., 52 ff.; W. Heisenberg, *Physics and Philosophy*, London, 1959, p. 49.

[35] *Ibid.*, p. 52; A. C. Benjamin, "Philosophy of the Sciences," *A History of Philosophical Systems*, V. Ferm, ed., New York, 1950, pp. 549f.

Before carrying the matter any further along this line, however, one should perhaps examine some of the assumptions of the scientist concerning the investigator himself.

Generally speaking, one seems to find that the average scientist believes himself to be a free and independent individual who may objectively investigate the temporal cosmos by means of scientifically developed techniques. He assumes that his intellect is "normal," i. e., without any functional maladjustment, which means that his own moral or religious views, and perhaps even his social relations, have no influence upon his interpretation of empirically gained data. Some of the social scientists, particularly historians, have at times disputed this outlook, but generally even they have adopted the attitude that if a man has a bias it comes from his social environment, not from any mental or religious maladjustment within his personality. Any bias should be overcome at least partially by adequate self-examination leading to self-consciousness.[36]

Man, therefore, when he investigates the temporal cosmos feels that his experience and measurements at least partially reveal reality to him. He classifies and arranges his experiences of phenomena according to type or property, attempting to seek a more general understanding of the laws governing them. Then he proceeds to formulate hypotheses and construct explanatory models, which he in turn checks by repeated references to the results of empirical research. Following this, he frames statements of general laws and eventually wide concepts.[37] In the views of some scientists, they have by this means come to a true understanding of temporal reality, while others hold that, even here, it again eludes them. But at the same time they all agree that as far

---

[36] Lerner, *op. cit.*, p. 10; P. W. Bridgman, *The Nature of Physical Theory*, Princeton, 1936, pp. 12 f.

[37] Kneale, *op. cit.*

as experience and measurement are concerned they have come to a knowledge of at least a segment of the universe which they can interpret truly and accurately, and concerning which they can generalize, even negatively.[38]

Thus the free individual can reach out to and acquire a knowledge of a certain amount of truth. But he does so in a law-governed world or in a chance-constructed world—however one looks at it—of which he himself forms a part. For this reason one might well raise the question of the value of such knowledge. Is it truly knowledge or understanding, and how can such knowledge be what they claim it to be? Is it not really but the haphazard working of the human imagination and its environment? It would seem that the claims so frequently advanced for the validity of the scientific method must find their grounds in a philosophy other than the positivism which the scientist usually advances, for positivism can truly accept nothing but individual experiences of chaos.

Added to this problem one finds that, only too frequently, the scientist states that he will consider as true only that which may come under the rules and investigations of the scientific method.[39] This would seem to exalt the scientific technique to an absolute standard for the discernment and acceptance of all truth. The logical aspect of man's experience then becomes the final arbiter in all discussions of the nature of truth; but if the temporal cosmos ultimately consists in chance, one finds it a little difficult to accept such a judge.[40] The scientist has attempted to deify a part of his own space-time conditioned personality in order to enable him to sit as ultimate interpreter of the universe.

---

[38] Lerner, *loc. cit.;* Caldin, *op. cit.*, pp. 19 ff.; Sir James Jeans, *Physics and Philosophy*, Cambridge, 1946, p. 189; P. W. Bridgman, "Science and Common Sense," *The Scientific Monthly* 79 (1954), pp. 32ff.

[39] Lerner, *op. cit.*, p. 13.

[40] Dooyeweerd, *Twilight*, pp. 8 ff.; *Critique*, II, 577.

Someone may at this point object that the author has not taken enough account of the new trends in science which, in delving into the sub-atomic structure of matter, have shown that the old positivistic empirical concepts no longer hold. Yet do they not? If one reads P. W. Bridgman's *The Nature of Physical Theory* and Sir Jeans' *Physics and Philosophy* both written in the 1930's and then turns to Heisenberg's *Physics and Philosophy* published in 1959 one discovers that while indeterminacy, the quantum theory, relativity and the like have become nuclei of the most recent thought, much the same point of view and attitude remain. True, the feeling of uncertainty about the possibility of really uncovering the nuclear components of atoms, and in particular of actually pin-pointing an electron in its movement, exercises a strong influence in the direction of caution. But still the fundamental humanistic assumptions tend to lie at the basis of contemporary physical science. *Plus ça change, plus c'est la même chose.*

The outcome of this position would seem to be a basic self-contradiction in scientific thought, which in turn destroys all possibility of scientific knowledge. Bertrand Russell's "A Free Man's Worship" would seem to demonstrate this conclusion admirably.[41] After asserting at the beginning that everything is chance and man the most peculiar of all accidents, he goes on to discuss man's intellectual activity and his accomplishments, apparently ignoring his own presuppositions. On a positivistic or humanistic scientific basis, the common approach of our own day, it would seem that one has no right to make any general statements, nor even to think of formulating general concepts, for they can mean nothing. And yet to carry out scientific research the most positivistic practitioner of the scientific method adopts philosophic presuppositions concerning both the nature of the temporal cosmos and himself, a procedure which flatly contradicts

[41] Published in *Mysticism and Logic*, London, 1953.

all his professed scientific positivism. Thus some other approach seems absolutely necessary.

The Christian Interpretation of the Scientific Method

As pointed out above, Calvin in the sixteenth century set forth the concept of a universe ruled by law, law divinely established and maintained in creation, providence and redemption. He held that the medieval concept of nature and grace had no value, since nature, God's handiwork, cannot be opposed to God's grace. Corruption, an alien force, has entered nature only by man's sin. Yet even sin could not possibly remove man from the law-structure of God's creation, so the law remains as the foundation for both the unity and diversity within the cosmos. This, man can see and understand only when he lays hold upon Jesus Christ as Saviour, who leads him into all truth, and enables him to grasp the fact that nature continues to remain God's creation, the revelation of divine sovereign wisdom and power.[42] Calvin thus laid the groundwork for a Christian concept of science and scientific method.[43] This pattern of thought we now wish to examine, in order to see what it tells concerning the Christian view of the scientific method.

In approaching this matter of the Christian interpretation of the scientific method, one must always keep in mind the fact that a Christian does not merely believe in certain abstract metaphysical or scientific theories. A Christian believes that he is a creature and a sinner saved from the wrath of God by the grace of God in Jesus Christ. By faith he has committed himself to Christ for eternal life. This gives him a completely new outlook on life, himself, and the world about him. He thus has

[42] Calvin, *Institutes*, bk. I, chaps. III-V; Dooyeweerd, *Critique*, I, p. 516.

[43] One of the best examples of his statement concerning this is to be found in his tract: *Adversus Astrologiam quam Iudiciariam Vocant* (1549).

a view of reality different from that of anyone who does not hold the same faith. His religion forms the foundation for his life, determining his whole perspective of outlook.

This is much more than a matter of church membership. It involves a total interpretation of the universe in which he lives, since it implies an ultimate interpretation of the origin, meaning and purpose of cosmic reality. For this reason, whether he recognizes it or not, he has a Christian approach to, and interpretation of, the scientific method. A Christian may, of course, not have a clear epistemological self-consciousness that enables him to think as consistently as a Christian should concerning such matters. Nevertheless, if he has experienced the regenerating power of the Holy Spirit, his basic outlook provides him with a position from which he may examine and analyze every approach to the study of the universe in which he lives.

To state the matter a little more carefully and exactly, the Christian knows God as the triune God: Father, Son and Holy Spirit, the One who is absolutely self-sufficient in power, wisdom, goodness and truth. He sees God, therefore, as the sovereign over the universe. This means that the ultimate environment of the temporal universe has a personal character. A naturalistic or irrationalistic concept of the ultimate character of reality can have no place in Christian thinking.

At once, of course, the problem arises as to how the Christian knows this. Is it by scientific investigation? To this the Christian must always answer that he knows God only by his own sovereign self-disclosure. God speaks to men by his works and by his Word, the Scriptures of the Old and New Testaments. He shows himself for what he is, and reveals himself by what he does. And yet man can never know God fully or completely, for the infinite and eternal One cannot be reduced to the finite temporal categories of the human mind. Moreover, man as a sinner, in rebellion against God and blinded by his own waywardness, does not wish to keep God as the sovereign in his mind. Thus only by divine revelation will man ever come to know God and so attain a true interpretation of temporal reality.[44]

As mentioned above, God reveals himself also by his works, which are in the first place creation and providence. He has originated and established all things according to his infinite power and wisdom. He has determined the structure of the temporal cosmos according to the pattern which he purposed within himself. This has resulted in the establishment and continuation of a creation which has unity within its diversities, a basic coherence as well as a basic multiplicity. Everything that exists in the universe exists by virtue of the laws of its structure and type which determine its inner nature, known to man only in temporal and perishable forms. Chance or even necessity has not produced the universe, but the wisdom of God who has already bestowed on all things the true interpretation.[45]

Of this creation man forms a part and he can never free himself from it. Since physically he has come from the dust of the ground, he is related to the whole of the rest of creation. At the same time, however, man stands above creation in that he is a personality. He possesses the power to analyze and synthesize his experiences, drawing from them general laws and principles. He has the capacity to mold and use the physical particulars of the cosmos for his own purposes and to organize himself and his fellows into social units, thus developing a culture. In all of this he proves himself different from, and superior to, the rest of creation.[46]

---

[44] *Cf.* Rom. 1:18 ff.

[45] Dooyeweerd, *Critique*, II, 547 ff.; Bavinck, *op. cit.*, pp. 90 ff.

[46] *Ibid.*, pp. 79 ff.; Dooyeweerd, *op. cit.*, II, 469, 553 ff. *Cf.* Calvin, *Commentaries on the First Book of Moses called Genesis*, 1:26; 9:2.

Why does man hold this position? To the Christian the answer lies in the fact that God created man in his own image, as a personality possessing true reason and knowledge, righteousness and holiness, although, since man always remains limited by the horizon of his own temporal experience of the cosmos, on a finite scale.[47] As God's vicegerent man received the commission to fill the earth and subdue it, a cultural obligation which no other creature can fulfill. Man could do so, however, by virtue of the structure of his divinely patterned personality or ego which possessed the intuitive capacity to understand his sensory impressions or experiences. As God created the temporal universe a law-structure consisting of numerous law-spheres with their own specific structures, so he created man with the intuitive capacity to relate those aspects of reality to himself. Thus man could obtain a true knowledge of the structure of temporal reality, and a true understanding of how it should be used.[48] But he did so on the basis of the fact that his intuition had a vertical as well as horizontal orientation. He saw all things in the light of the sovereign God. Thinking analogically, he thought God's thoughts after him.

The process of man's thinking analogically to God's true interpretation and understanding begins with pretheoretical experience and intuition. God has created man so that his organs of sensory perception present him with experiences which correspond to objective reality in all its individuality.[49] But these experiences, or the things which he knows by them, do not appear in his consciousness as equations, or even as scientific structures. Rather they impinge upon his consciousness as concrete things and events in their full totality. For

---

[47] Dooyeweerd, *op. cit.*, II, 554 f.; Bavinck, *op. cit.*, pp. 53 f.

[48] Dooyeweerd, *op. cit.*, II, 475 ff., 547 ff.

[49] *Ibid.*, I, 561 f.; II, 557 ff.; *Twilight*, pp. 6 ff.

instance, because one thirsts one takes a drink of water, but one does not have a sense perception of H_2O with various other chemical, physical, biological and economic attributes. One experiences the water as a totality which takes away the dryness of the throat and satisfies the body's craving for more fluid. One knows water in this way, but such knowledge does not bring with it scientific or theoretical understanding. It represents what Dooyeweerd calls "naive experience," which, although not scientific knowledge, must lie at the basis of all subsequent theoretical analysis.[50]

Naive, pre-theoretical intuition of the temporal cosmos makes distinctions, as, for instance, when one differentiates between water and gasoline by certain sensory criteria, but these distinctions one cannot term "scientific." Scientific knowledge consists in abstraction, by which one employing certain scientific hypotheses and techniques abstracts chosen aspects from the experience of specific phenomena of reality. The chemist, for instance, analyzes water by means of electrolysis into two atoms of hydrogen and one of oxygen, and the physicist studies the problem of the freezing or vaporization of water. Other scientists interested in its biological, physiological, economic or social uses or its practical importance on the basis of the work of chemists and physicists, deal with other aspects. In all of these cases the scientist tends to abstract, so that no one abstraction really represents the whole truth, for abstraction means onesidedness and artificial isolation.[51] This takes place not by some mechanical means but by the human person, the rationalizing "I," who has the ability to stand back from his experiences of reality and so to examine and analyze them that he obtains something of an under-

[50] *Ibid.*, II, 468 f.; 557 f.; *Twilight*, pp. 13 ff.; Bavinck, *op. cit.*, pp. 56 ff.

[51] Dooyeweerd, *Critique*, II, 469 ff., 575; *Twilight*, pp. 12 ff.

standing of an abstract aspect of the structure of temporal reality.

Because of the fact that the scientist's logical, abstract knowledge of the temporal horizon always remains bound to sense experience, he may never separate his theoretical from his pre-theoretical intuition of the temporal cosmos. He may never become a rationalist attempting merely, by deduction from general principles, to attain a true theoretical understanding of an aspect of reality. He must continually go back to his concrete experiences in order to check all his scientific theorizing. Thus induction cannot but be the basic scientific method. All theories, all interpretations, he must test repeatedly by the phenomena of temporal reality.[52] For this very reason, therefore, one may never say that a scientific understanding of one aspect of reality or of the "scientific method" enables one to reach out to absolute truth, nor even to understand nature-in-itself. Scientific endeavor is limited to the temporal horizon of experience and deals with abstracted aspects of man's experience of the phenomena within that horizon.[53]

At the same time, however, an aspect of phenomena abstracted from the coherence of temporal reality does not constitute wholly true knowledge even of that one aspect. It cannot possibly exist in isolation from its total environment, and this limitation applies not only to the phenomenon known but also to the knower. The possibility of man's developing a special science depends upon the existence of a certain type of temporal reality, one over which law rules. Moreover, the knowledge of this world implies, indeed necessitates, specific relationships between the scientist and the phenomena which he investigates. But even attempts to understand a special science by linking it to the rest of temporal reality do not suffice, for temporal reality is not self-explanatory. True

[52] *Ibid.*, pp. 18 f.; *Critique*, II, 4 ff.
[53] *Ibid.*, II, 561; *Twilight*, p. 6.

scientific knowledge comes only when men see themselves and the phenomena of the cosmos in the light of eternity, from the perspective of Jesus Christ the creator, the sustainer and redeemer of men. To the Christian, here alone lies the source of the true understanding of science, for only in this faith can one justify the use of the scientific method.[54]

At this point, however, one faces the inescapable fact that although men do not interpret reality in this way, they still do achieve much in the scientific field by means of the scientific method. How does the Christian explain this, especially as he himself insists that any explanation must stick to the empirical facts?

To the Christian the answer lies in the fall of man into sin and God's redemption. Although man's finitude would keep him from having absolutely comprehensive knowledge of the temporal cosmos, his knowledge as far as it might go would be true, for he would not only have a proper insight into the law-structure of the cosmos and in particular of his particular area of investigation, but he would see all things in their true relationships to God as creator and sustainer. Man, however, has refused to accept God as God, insisting that no prior interpretation of the universe exists and that he can attain to absolute knowledge by stressing one aspect of experience, usually the logical-scientific, so that it becomes the guide to *all* truth. Whatever lies beyond its range remains mysterious for man and for God also, if there be a God. This outlook stems from the fact that sin consists in personal alienation from God, so that when man comes to study the temporal cosmos his eyes refuse to see that he must always take God into account if he would obtain true knowledge.[55] Hence man's error.

---

[54] Dooyeweerd, *Critique*, I, 561 f.; II, 504 ff.; Bavinck, *op. cit.*, p. 106 f.

[55] Dooyeweerd, *Critique*, II, 547 ff., 573 f.

How does this error manifest itself? Man seeks independence from God, endeavoring to attain to creativity in his own right. He falls victim to Satan's temptation: "Ye shall be as gods, discerning good from evil" (Gen. 3:5). He therefore begins with himself as an independent thinking being whose reason is the standard of truth. In this way, even though he may not deny some god's existence, he does reject the idea of the necessity of his absolute subjection to the deity. Rather he interprets the world as though he and it stand alongside his god as independent entities. Commencing his thinking from a humanistic presupposition, he cannot but end by asserting his autonomy in his interpreting and using this temporal reality.[56]

At this point the non-Christian runs into serious difficulties. While proclaiming his freedom from philosophical presuppositions in his employment of the scientific method, he nevertheless usually assumes hidden positivistic presuppositions coupled with a belief in natural order which in turn hardly agree with his positivistic, purely experimental approach to realtiy. To think scientifically he must accept a concept of law-coherence within the temporal universe, which in turn implies ultimate rationality as the universe's foundation. If he cannot know aspects of the universe truly without any reference to ultimates, or by positing ultimate chance or mystery, the assumption of a basic rationale to all things would seem required. Whether he likes it or not the unbelieving scientist finds himself forced to bow to the reality of the law-structure of the universe in order to be a scientist, which seems to constitute a denial of his prior assumption of his own and his world's autonomy.[57] This would seem to destroy any possibility of accepting the validity of his non-Christian presuppositions.

---

[53] *Ibid.*, II, 552, 581 f.; *Twilight*, p. 59; Bavinck, *op. cit.*, pp. 98 ff. Caldin, *op. cit.*, pp. 9 ff., in discussing the scientific method, makes this very clear.

[57] *Ibid.*, pp. 15ff.; Dooyeweerd, *Critique*, I, 550 f.; II, 571 ff.

For man to employ logically and consistently the scientific method, he must come to see it in its basic coherence with the rest of temporal reality, and this he does only when he looks at all things in the light of eternity. But such light comes by no other means than the grace of God which speaks to us by his Word and Spirit concerning Jesus Christ as Saviour and Lord. When by the effectual calling of God one comes to faith in Christ, one has become a new person, not merely ethically but in one's fundamental "religious center" which determines the individual's outlook on the whole of his life and experience. This produces a change in one's interpretation of the temporal cosmos, so that one no longer attempts to elevate a single aspect, particularly the logical-scientific, to the place of absolute truth but realizes that one knows the truth only when one sees it in the perspective of Christ who thus becomes "the new root of our cosmos."[58] Although sin would have shattered our cosmos, God has maintained it and redeemed it in Christ the source of all true knowledge.

At this point, an important question arises, one which many Christians seem to ignore. If indeed one uses the scientific method properly only if one is a Christian, what about all the myriads of non-Christian, even atheistic, scholars, who also use it and to apparently good effect? Does their work have no value? Are all their achievements purely illusory? From listening to some Christians talk, one might well think that this is the case. Such an attitude, however, by no means represents a truly Christian point of view.

The Christian purview takes into account both human apostasy and divine purpose in creation. To accomplish his purpose and to make his special redemptive grace effective in this world, God, by his common grace bestowed upon all men, has restrained the effects of sin.

---

[58] *Ibid.*, I, 522 f.; II, 561 ff.; *Twilight*, pp. 42 f., 54.

"The sense of deity," of which Calvin speaks, still remains even within the most agnostic mind, giving the unbelieving scientist the assurance that he may know the temporal universe rationally. Thus although unbelievers may remain blind to the vertical significance of temporal reality, if they do but "capitulate to the temporal Divine order," they can gain a relatively true understanding of the states of affairs here and now. Thus in all interpretations and philosophies one finds relative truths; but these become ultimate falsehoods when interpreted immanently and subjectively. Forced by the structure of reality to acknowledge its law-governed pattern, they achieve much, but frequently they then go on to extrapolate their findings to provide an explanation for the whole of reality, ending up in a slough of chance or ultimate ineluctable mystery.[59]

As the Christian, therefore, studies this matter of the scientific method in relation to his own faith, he need not fear it nor feel that as a Christian he must disregard the discoveries and achievements of those unbelievers who have gone before. Successive generations of scholars have built up a structure of knowledge in the past which itself has become part of man's temporal horizon of experience. God has given to many great gifts and capacities which they have employed to investigate the relationships and structures of temporal reality, thereby making marvelous and astonishing discoveries concerning its character. These discoveries the Christian must not despise or disdain, but use them as God intends, to obtain a greater understanding of his power and glory. True, scientists may commence from a wrong idea of the nature of the universe, ignoring or denying that they may explain it truly in the light of God's self-revelation alone. Nevertheless, the Christian must recognize that the scientific method holds good because God is sovereign.[60]

---

[59] *Ibid.*, pp. 54 f.; *Critique*, I, 522 f.; II, 571 ff.

When the unbeliever uses it he is basically inconsistent, and when he makes discoveries of truth he does so, not by virtue of his intellectual autonomy, but by the grace of God which preserves both the law-structure of the universe and some vestiges of the image of God in man.

In the past most Christians, when interpreting both Scripture and the world of nature, have followed a method ultimately derived from the thought of Aristotle. They have, for instance, sought to interpret the Bible, particularly in its reference to natural phenomena, along Scholastic and Aristotelian lines. This Dooyeweerd with good reason terms "oppressive to the Christian faith and to honest scientific investigation."[61] Even many Reformed scholars have fallen into the same trap, not infrequently attempting by scholastic reasoning to refute new theoretical or scientific ideas which have conflicted with traditional scholastic interpretations of the Bible. The Christian scholar, however, cannot submit himself uncritically to any philosophy, even though put forward by Christians, but must on true Christian grounds prove all things and hold fast that which is good.

What implications arise then out of this? In a world largely dominated by science and the scientific method, what attitude must the Christian take? A mere confession of faith or telling of "what Christ means to me," important as Christian witness of this type may be, hardly meets the situation. The Christian, in obedience to God's cultural mandate to man, has the abiding responsibility of understanding and knowing temporal reality scientifically. This of course has always been the case, but in our own day and age it has become even more imperative. Christians must not only involve themselves in their world, but they should in particular turn their attention to the scientific spheres in order that they may demonstrate clearly and dramatically that only if man

[60] *Ibid.*, II, 576 ff.

[61] *Ibid.*, I, 510.

knows the sovereign God through Jesus Christ, can he truly depend upon and use the scientific method as a means of understanding the world in which he lives.

CHAPTER III

NATURAL SCIENCE IN SIXTEENTH-CENTURY CALVINISTIC THOUGHT

In recent years historians of science have pushed the beginnings of the so-called "scientific revolution" from the middle of the seventeenth century into the last half of the sixteenth, and have even traced some of its roots as far as Robert Grosseteste of the thirteenth.[1] Yet, as A. C. Crombie has admitted, these same historians are at a loss to provide a unified explanation for the fact that the new scientific outlook appears to have had its beginnings in the latter half of the 1500's. He has suggested various reasons such as economic and social conditions, while others have mentioned new patterns of thought that came into conflict with the accepted humanism of the Renaissance and similar intellectual movements.[2] In general, however, the interpreters of the scientific development have either ignored or specifically denied the influence of the Reformation, a movement widespread and influential in the very geographic areas where natural science later attained some of its greatest achievements.[3] For this reason we will endeavor to set forth some of the scientific concepts which Calvin and his followers developed and which seem to have contributed to the seventeenth-century scientific development, in this way forming a stage on the way to Newton's *Principia*.

Historians of science have stated more than once that the scientific movement of the sixteenth century

[1] Cf. A. C. Crombie, *Robert Grosseteste and the Origins of Experimental Science, 1100-1700* (Oxford, 1953).

[2] *Augustine to Galileo* (London, 1957), p. 275.

[3] H. Haydn, *The Counter-Renaissance* (New York, 1960), p. 245, declares that Luther and Calvin both disliked the arts and sciences since they laid all their stress upon salvation, while W. C. D. Dampier-Whetham, *A History of Science* (New York, 1930), p. 118, believes that the only importance of the Reformation for science was that it unintentionally broke ecclesiastical control over European thought.

brought no sudden change in thought, but only carried the medieval and Renaissance thinking somewhat farther.[4] While this point of view in some ways has considerable truth, one must always bear in mind that medieval scientific endeavor from 1250 on usually followed the lead of Aristotle in stressing the metaphysical background of physics by laying its stress on final causes, in searching for qualitative rather than quantitative attributes, and in employing the form-substance dialectical explanation for nature which soon came to be equated with the theological grace-nature motive.[5] Although the work of Grosseteste, Roger Bacon, and their followers pointed in the direction of a more empirical, experimental type of method, their influence died out under the impact of Renaissance humanism.[6] The humanists revived the study of the classical scientific texts and commentaries, but generally speaking they did little to stimulate an interest in what one today would call scientific investigation.[7] Even Vesalius and Copernicus, although they had

---

[4] H. Brown, "The Renaissance Historians of Science," *Studies in the Renaissance* (New York), VII (1960), 27ff., holds that the scientific revolution "cannot be said to begin much before the very end of the sixteenth century, and it dates properly from the seventeenth" (p. 36). Cf. also A. R. Hall, *The Scientific Revolution, 1500-1800* (London, 1954) pp. 68ff.; N. W. Gilbert, *The Renaissance Concept of Method* (New York, 1960), pp. 223f.

[5] T. F. Torrance, "The Influence of Reformed Thought on the Development of Scientific Method," *Dialogue: A Journal of Theology,* II (1963), 42; E. A. Burtt, *The Metaphysical Foundations of Modern Science* (rev. ed., New York, 1931), pp. 17ff.; J. Dillenberger, *Protestant Thought and Natural Science* (London, 1961), p. 23; P. O. Kristeller, *Renaissance Thought* (New York, 1961), p. 31.

[6] Crombie, *Grosseteste*, pp. 290ff.; Kristeller, *op. cit.*, p. 33. W. J. Ong, *Ramus Method and the Decay of Dialogue* (Harvard University Press, 1958), p. 142, believes that many of the Roman Catholic theologians of the sixteenth century were beginning to enter the field of natural science but the Reformation forced them back to biblical studies. This would hardly seem to have been general.

[7] The principal Renaissance contribution came in the form of a revived study of "method," on classical lines, but the humanists never devised a "scientific method" as such. Their main stress lay upon the study of classical texts. Gilbert, *op. cit.*, p. 231; Kristeller, *op. cit.*, pp. 40ff.; cf. R. Hooykaas, "Humanisme, science et reform," *Free University Quarterly*, Amsterdam, V (1958), 171.

largely broken from the ancient traditions, still showed little appreciation of the modern point of view.[8]

Probably the chief stimulus to change in accepted interpretations of nature came as a result of practical technical discoveries and inventions. The medieval Scholar had thought primarily in terms of arranging a curriculum for teaching, but increasingly craftsmen, surgeons, navigators and the like, seeking some limited, practical objective which would help with their work, discovered new facts and invented new machines or instruments. Theoretical interpretation then had to accommodate itself to these novelties which because of their increase became something of a problem in the sixteenth century.[9] Aristotle could not be discharged from his place of predominance until some new interpretation, as all-inclusive as his, had been established. Yet at the same time, he and even more his disciples were proving less and less satisfactory as interpreters of the new knowledge. Consequently, the more advanced "scientific thinkers" began to reject the Aristotelian pattern of the universe.[10] Of these quite a number turned to the pre-Aristotelian philosophers for their explanations as did Paracelsus, while others such as William Gilbert employed a good many ideas derived from magic and naturalistic mysticism.[11] And yet neither of these approaches met the need for an all-inclusive theory, with the result that others like

---

[8] This statement would not in any sense deny the value of their contributions, but when analyzed, their work did not follow nor did it have as its mainspring a modern "scientific" approach. Vesalius seems to have regarded his work primarily as a matter of technique while Copernicus sought an explanation different from that of Ptolemy because the latter's system did not manifest the simplicity which Copernicus thought should be implicit in nature. M. Boas, *The Scientific Renaissance, 1450-1630* (London, 1962), p. 77; Hall, *op. cit.*, chap. II; Hooykaas, *op. cit.*, p. 177; Burtt, *op. cit.*, pp. 38ff.; H. Butterfield, *The Origins of Modern Science* (London, 1950), pp. 22ff.

[9] Butterfield, *ibid.*, pp. 210ff.; Ong. *op. cit.*, pp. 224ff.; Gilbert, *op. cit.*, p. 230.

[10] Boas, *op. cit.*, pp. 238ff.; Kristeller, *op. cit.*, p. 44.

[11] Hooykaas, *op. cit.*, p. 171; Boas, *op. cit.*, p. 190.

Peter Ramus, in his early work, although strongly anti-Aristotelian had no adequate system to put in the place of the accepted interpretation.[12]

Because of this situation, the Protestant Reformation, particularly its Calvinistic phase, had a special appeal for the philosophically homeless students of nature. The primary reason for this was Luther's and particularly Calvin's opposition to the whole medieval-Aristotelian Scholastic synthesis with its rationalistic attempt to place everything in nature in logical and hierarchial relationships.[13] Furthermore, the rejection of the idea of church control and the stress upon vocation even in scientific studies no doubt also had their influence.[14] Consequently, one finds that a number of sixteenth-century "scientific" practitioners, thinkers and writers, such as Peter Ramus,[15] Bernard Palissy, [16] Ambrose Paré,[17] and

---

[12] Boas, *ibid.*, p. 238. Peter Ramus, in his pre-Protestant days before 1562, seems to have sought a philosophic system in dialectic by which he could co-ordinate all his thought, but he never seems to have felt that he had achieved his aim. *Vide infra.*

[13] A. S. Nash, *The University and the Modern World* (New York, 1944), pp. 62f.; Torrance, *op. cit.*, p. 42; Hooykaas, *op. cit.*, pp. 169, 263.

[14] Nash, *op. cit.*, p. 64f.; A. Lecerf, *Etudes Calvinistes* (Paris, 1949), pp. 116ff., points out that "pour le Calvinisme, il n'y a rien de profane que le mal." Consequently, the study of natural science might well be a man's God-given vocation, in which he would fulfill his calling as much as the minister did in his.

[15] Peter Ramus (1515-1572) became an influential philosopher and "methodologist" in the Université de France. W. J. Ong feels that his influence led to sterility of thought, but Ong does not seriously consider the changes which came in his views after his conversion to Protestantism, particularly his insistence upon his freedom over against the Aristotelianism of the Sorbonne. He was killed on the third day of the Massacre of St. Bartholomew's Eve.

[16] Bernard Palissy (1510-1590), a potter of Saintes, by dint of experimentation succeeded in producing an enamel similar to that of Majolica. He became a special favorite of the French court and so escaped the St. Bartholomew's Eve massacre. He died in the Bastille for his Protestantism in 1590.

[17] Ambrose Paré (1510-1590) became probably the most famous French surgeon of his day. He also escaped the Massacre of St. Bartholomew's Eve through royal protection. He was noted for his empirical approach to matters medical. Cf. F. R. Packard, *Life and Times of Ambrose Paré* (New York, 1921), pp. 80ff.

Francis Bacon[18] accepted Calvinism which in turn seems to have stimulated them to further efforts in their studies.[19] To understand this, however, one must see how Calvinism provided them with the structure of thought of which they felt in need and how they employed it in their scientific thinking.

The Nature of Nature

Calvin as a theologian did not spend much of his time discussing natural science, but both his doctrinal and his exegetical works reveal a very well-defined view of nature and of man's understanding of it. In this, his doctrine of creation holds pride of place for by his stress upon the fact that everything beyond God comes from the divine creative activity in Jesus Christ, he rejects any idea of one "great chain of being." Thus, even in its ideal structure, creation has a qualitatively different essence from that of God.[20] Neither are form nor substance, universals nor particulars, co-eternal with God. Rather there exist two levels of reality, the Eternal and the temporal, the uncreated and the created, and though man made in the image of God spiritually and intellectually stands half-

---

[18] Francis Bacon in the history of science is not usually considered as particularly religious owing to the fact that his confession of faith is often ignored. Yet when one reads his statements in his *Advancement of Learning* and similar works in conjunction with his confession, one can see that a strong Calvinism colored all his scientific thinking. For Bacon's confession see *Works*, ed. J. Spedding and R. L. Ellis (London, 1870), VII, 215ff.

[19] Both Calvin and Ramus more than once referred to the fact that there seemed to be a relationship between the rise of Protestantism and the growth of the knowledge of natural science. J. Calvin, "Advertissement contre l'astrologie judiciare," *Opera Omnia*, ed. G. Baum *et al.* (Brunswick, 1868), VII, 516; Hooykaas, *op. cit.*, p. 252.

[20] J. Calvin, *Commentary on Genesis* (Grand Rapids, 1948), 1, xxxi: "le premier livre de Moyse mérite d'estre tenu pour un thresor inestimable, lequel pour le moins nous donne certitude infallible de la creation du monde: san lequelle, nous ne sommes pas dignes que la terre nous soustierne." Cf. also J. Bohatec, *Budé und Calvin* (Graz, 1950, p. 269; E. A. Dowey, *The Knowledge of God in Calvin's Theology* (New York, 1952), pp. 73ff.

way between, he still forms part of the dependent, space-time condition reality.[21]

Yet with all his stress upon the difference between the Creator and the creature, Calvin never adopted a deistic interpretation of reality.[22] God continually orders, upholds and governs creation by the "secret power" of his Holy Spirit who brought order out of original chaos and who keeps all things in existence even now. Calvin also insisted that all things operate usually according to the laws with which God has endowed nature and which the Holy Spirit continually maintains and activates.[23] Only on special occasions, i.e., on occasions of special revelation or special redemptive action, does God act directly, i.e., above or contrary to secondary causes.[24] Thus law, established and continued by God's Spirit, binds the whole of creation together.

It can hardly cause any surprise, therefore, that Calvin insisted that the created-temporal reality forms one vast system, not of substantial forms but of phenomena and laws. More than once Calvin devoted his attention to the magnificent order of the whole of the universe which operates without the slightest sign of confusion according to the laws which God sustains and governs at all times. The "ordo naturae" to Calvin forms one grand machine which manifests the wonderful divine wisdom, power and goodness. Contrary to what many seem to think, therefore, nature in his mind was something to be

---

[21] Torrance, *op. cit.*, p. 41; Bohatec, *op. cit.*, pp. 264f.; Hall, *op. cit.*, p. xvi.

[22] Hall, *ibid.*, p. xvii.

[23] Calvin's views on God's providential care of nature through the Holy Spirit appear in many places in his commentaries although he seems to sum up the whole matter in his words concerning Acts 17:28: "For the power of the Spirit is spread abroad throughout all the parts of the world, that it may preserve them in their state; that he may minister unto the heaven and earth that force and vigour which we see, and motion to all living creatures." Cf. also: Ps. 19:1, 2; Jeremiah 10:12, 13; Isaiah 40:22; *Institutes of the Christian Religion,* I, xvi, 4ff.

[24] W. Keusche, *Das Wirken des Heiligen Geistes nach Calvin* (Göttingen, 1957), pp. 25ff.; "Advertissement," *Opera,* VII, 532.

considered and enjoyed, for it radiates the glory of the sovereign God.[25]

To summarize Calvin's thought and to show how he applied it, one should examine his views on astrology to which he gave expression in 1549 by the publication of *Admonitio Adversus Astrologiam, quam Iudiciariam Vocant*. In this tractate he maintains that the study of the heavens by man is a proper and legitimate occupation, as long as man limits himself to the study of the motions and relationships of the celestial bodies. In his statements concerning this aspect of "astrology" he shows no sign of ever having heard of Copernicus, which is hardly surprising seeing that he wrote only four years after the publication of the *De Revolutionibus*. When he turns to the judicial astrologers, he bases his criticism primarily upon empirical evidence, rejecting all ideas of heavenly intelligences, the harmony of the spheres and the difference of heavenly from terrestrial substances. While he accepts generally Ptolemy's system of crystalline spheres his views differ radically from those of Dante as expressed in *The Banquet*. Moreover, although the heavenly host may influence man's body in some ways, they have no control over his actions or his fortunes. God alone governs by the laws of his universe.[26]

All of those who professed to be followers of Calvin during the forty years following his death in 1564 did not succeed in remaining as free from Aristotelian influences

---

[25] *Institutes*, I, xiv, 20, 21; Ps. 104: 1-4; Ps. 19:2; Dowey, *op. cit.*, p. 66; Krusche, *op. cit.*, pp. 15ff. "Therefore, if any smatterer in philosophy, with a view to ridicule the simplicity of our faith, contend that such a variety of colours [in a rainbow] is the natural result of the refraction of the solar rays on an opposite cloud, we must immediately acknowledge it, but we may smile at his stupidity in not acknowledging God as the Lord and Governor of nature, who uses all the elements according to his nature for the promotion of His own glory." *Institutes*, IV, xiv, 18.

[26] Calvin's tractate also appeared for popular consumption in a French translation in the same year as "L'avertissement contre l'astrologie judiciaire." His views on astrology also appear at appropriate places in his biblical commentaries. Cf. Bohatec, *op. cit.*, pp. 268ff.; Lecerf, *op. cit.*, pp. 119f.

as did he. Beza, Calvin's successor in Geneva, and many others accepted whole-heartedly Aristotle's guidance in matters scientific.[27] And yet even convinced Aristotelians could hardly follow Aristotle entirely, as long as they maintained Calvin's doctrine of creation, which most of them did. Jerome Zanche, an Italian theologian at Heidelberg University, for instance, in his *De Operibus Dei intra Spaciam Sex Diebus Creatis* written around 1570, spends considerable time attacking Aristotle's views on the eternality of matter, and even alters the philosopher's teachings concerning the relation of form and substance by insisting that diversity and distinctions in the natural world arise solely out of the sovereign creative will of God.[28] Similarly Peter Ramus in his *Scholae Mathematicae* (1569) stresses that God had created all things, particularly the heavens, on a mathematical pattern.[29] In the same way Bernard Palissy sought in his art to reproduce "the works of God as they came from his hands,"[30] while Francis Bacon continually refers to God's creation of all things, and like the others takes for granted Calvin's "two level" interpretation of all reality.[31]

When one studies the thought of Calvin's followers with regard to providence, natural law and secondary causes one finds again rather complete unanimity. Zanche spends much time setting forth the Reformed doctrine of providence as the basis for the idea of natural law and the validity of secondary causes;[32] while in Palissy one even hears echoes of the very phraseology and examples

---

[27] Dillenberger, *op. cit.*, p. 62; Hooykaas, *op. cit.*, 177.

[28] 2nd ed., Hanover, 1597, Part I, Lib. i, chap. iii.

[29] Hooykaas, *op. cit.*, pp. 250ff.

[30] A. Dumesnil, *Bernard Palissy* (Paris, 1851), pp. 38ff., 53; H. Morley, *Palissy the Potter* (London, 1852), II, 240ff.; *Les Oeuvres de Bernard Palissy*, ed. Anatole France (Paris, 1880), pp. 106ff.

[31] *The Advancement of Learning*, ed., G. W. Kitchin (London, 1915), p. 8.

[32] *De Operibus*, Pt. I, Lib. I, cap. iii; Pt. II, Lib. II, cap. iv.

cited by Calvin.[33] Bacon sums the whole matter up when, after pointing out that final causes are matters properly metaphysical and physical causes relate only to this world, he insists that "neither doth this [distinction] call in question, or derogate from Divine Providence, but highly confirm and exalt it."[34] To these men as to Calvin the relationships of things arose out of natural law, created and sustained by God's sovereign power.

Similarly they all laid great stress upon the fact that this world of nature formed one vast machine, a term used numerous times by Zanche and others. Even the smallest and most vile phenomena of creation form part of the great whole.[35] Palissy in his pottery continually modelled his ornaments on lizards, molluscs and fish, because he held that these all form part of God's great and grand design of creation.[36] In this way the concept of "system" dominated their understanding of nature of which no part was too small or too unimportant for consideration and study. On the other hand, they never accepted the idea of a static universe. Zanche insisted more than once that the physical universe continually moves forward to the completion of God's purpose, while Palissy held that it did so by natural processes as revealed by the fact that many rocks were laid down by both sedimentary and volcanic action.[37] Ramus and Bacon likewise subscribed to this continual purposive movement of all things physical.[38] But always the movement arose out of God's action and according to his natural laws.

What did these men hold concerning the heavens? Most of them accepted completely Calvin's views on

---

[33] Dumesnil, *op. cit.*, pp. 50ff.; Morley, *op. cit.*, pp. 133, 140, 158.

[34] *Advancement*, p. 98.

[35] *De Operibus*, Pt. I, Lib. I, cap. iii, p. 54, "Nihil vero tam vile atque exiguum esse in mundo, quod non suum habeat usum ad totius machinae, tamquam totius corporis conservationem, ornatum, formam."

[36] *Oeuvres*, pp. 231ff.; 446ff.

[37] *De Operibus*, Pt. I, Lib. I, cap. iii, p. 54; Morley, *op. cit.*, p. 158.

[38] Hooykaas, *op. cit.*, pp. 232ff.; Bacon, *Advancement*, p. 93.

astrology, rejecting any mystical or magical influence of the heavenly bodies and denying any such things as heavenly intelligences or spheric harmonies.[39] With regard to Copernicus' theories those who dealt with the subject seem to have been divided.[40] Zanche, for instance, took the Ptolemaic structure for granted.[41] Bacon seems to have put Ptolemy and Copernicus on a par, for although he held no brief for Ptolemy he felt that Copernicus had endeavored to over-simplify matters and both theories would have to await further confirmation.[42] Ramus, on the other hand, supported the Copernican ideas largely because he rejected Ptolemy's epicycles as too complicated, but as a result of Osiander's unsigned introduction to the *De Revolutionibus* he also criticized Copernicus strongly for setting forth his theory merely as a mathematical hypothesis for calculation. He felt that he should have maintained that it conformed to the facts.[43] In general one may say that with their view of the universe and the sovereignty of God over all, they had no need to worry if this planet did cease to be the physical center of all things.[44]

To the Calvinist, then, nature is not a servant to be exploited or a temptress to be avoided. Rather, God has created nature that he might show forth his glory which man alone may recognize. Man with a "natural" body, but created in the image of God, has received the commis-

---

[39] Cf. Zanche, *De Operibus*, Pt. II, Lib. VI, cap. ii; Bacon, *Advancement*, p. 29.

[40] As pointed out by Boas, *op. cit.*, pp. 101ff., Copernicus' theory did not receive unanimous support before the first quarter of the seventeenth century. Tycho Brahe, Guillaume du Bartas, Jean Bodin, Michel de Montaigne and John Donne all either rejected Copernicus or had very great doubts concerning his views.

[41] *De Operibus*, Pt. I, Lib. I, cap. II, p. 19.

[42] Bacon, *Advancement*, p. 104.

[43] Hooykaas, *op. cit.*, pp. 230.

[44] Calvin, while holding "that the circuit of the heavens is finite, and that the earth like a little globe is placed in the centre," also held that "in comparison with the boundless waste which remains empty, the heaven and earth occupy but a small space." *Commentary on Genesis*, The Argument.

sion of God to "subdue the world and rule over it." The Calvinist saw nature as something objective to himself which he must endeavor to understand and use in order that he might truly fulfil his task upon earth. This provided him with an effective stimulus to scientific investigation.[45]

The Science of Nature

As pointed out at the beginning of this chapter, science in the Middle Ages and Renaissance had, despite some opposition, largely accepted Aristotle as its guide. This meant that not only his description of the physical universe but also his deductive, syllogistic method as the only proper method for scientific study, dominated men's minds. This was the heritage of the sixteenth century and in many cases even those who rebelled against the medieval theological and religious outlook continued to adhere closely to Aristotle's scientific method.[46] Yet as in the case of the explanation of nature, the practice of scientific method during the century kept well ahead of the theory. The craftsmen and artisans as well as many others working in practical affairs began to develop increasingly an empirical approach for which they needed theoretical justification and explanation.[47] Aristotelianism did not provide the answer, but Calvinism offered a rationale which opened the way towards seventeenth-century developments.

In order to understand Calvin's influence on the scientific method, one must look first at his theological technique. Seeking to reform the church, he turned back to the original Christian source, the biblical text, which he believed to be the Word of God. His method of approach to the Scriptures was basically empirical for he rejected

---

[45] *Ibid.;* Bohatec, *op. cit.*, p. 269; Dumesnil, *op. cit.*, p. 64.

[46] Hooykaas, *op. cit.*, p. 177; Dillenberger, *op. cit.*, p. 62; C. Waddington, *Ramus, sa vie, ses écrits et ses opinions* (Paris, 1855), pp. 190ff.

[47] Hooykaas, *op. cit.*, p. 257.

all speculation and all philosophizing in favor of a strict grammatico-historical exegesis under the guidance of God's Spirit, which limits one to what the text actually says.[48] This method has wielded a strong influence on Calvinists down to the present day, but in the late sixteenth century it completely dominated their thinking. Even as Aristotelian such as Zanche adhered rigorously to it, while Ramus and Bacon made it the very heart of their approach to Holy Writ.[49]

Calvin, however, did not stop with a theological method, for he held that God also revealed himself in his works of creation and providence. These latter man comes to know not by studying the Scriptures, but by investigating nature itself.[50] Here the two-level theory of reality came into play, for he insisted that one must investigate the things of this earth by appropriate mundane means, the only limitation being that unless men see this earth "in the light of eternity," by which he means in the perspective of faith in Christ, they will neither understand it truly nor use it properly.[51] At the same time he also insisted that since God is the creator and sustainer man can never understand all his works; he can only analyze their relationships and material causes, recognizing that even the *ordo naturae* because of

---

[48] Calvin's attitude to the writings of Dionysius the Areopagite illustrates his approach: "No one will deny that Dionysius, whoever he was, subtly and skilfully discussed many things in his *Celestial Hierarchy*. But if anyone studied it more closely, he will find it for the most part nothing but talk. . . . If you read that book, you would think a man fallen from heaven recounted, not what he had learned, but what he had seen with his own eyes." (*Institutes*, I, xiv, 34), Cf. Haydn, *op. cit.*, p. 212; Lecerf, *op. cit.*, pp. 121f.

[49] Bacon, *Advancement*, pp. 209ff., 214f.; "Religious Meditations," *Works*, VII, 252ff.; Gilbert, *op. cit.*, p. 110; Hooykaas, *op. cit.*, p. 287.

[50] "Avertissement," *Opera*, VII, 523f., 529f., Cf. also his comments on Ps. 148:3; 1 Cor. 1:17. Lecerf, *op. cit.*, p. 123.

[51] *Instruction in Faith* (1537), ed. P. T. Fuhrmann (Philadelphia, 1949), p. 20; Comment on 1 Cor. 1:20 Dowey, *op. cit.*, pp. 77, 131 ff.; Bohatec, *op. cit.*, pp. 265ff.

its divine origin is never wholly subject to human rational analysis.[52]

In the light of this interpretation how did Calvin regard non-Christian scientific endeavors? The answer to this question is that although he held that by the Fall man had lost all capacity for the knowledge of both God and the creation, God in his grace through the Holy Spirit does give even to unbelievers certain gifts by which they may investigate and understand this world.[53] This knowledge and ability he never said was "natural" but came from God's special benevolence, so that even the Christian had to acknowledge and thank God for what he calls the ancient philosophers' "fine observation and careful description of nature."[54] In this way he accepted all scientific investigation as God-given for the use and profit of man.[55]

Here again, once they had accepted his basic theological presuppositions, even Calvin's most Aristotelian disciples found it necessary to follow. Zanche repeatedly praises the study of nature as the study of God's work, although he has as his objective the establishment of a perfect science such as that set forth in Aristotle's *Physics*.[56] Similarly, Ramus made repeated calls for the study of nature, holding that man's "natural reason" if

---

[52] *Instruction*, p. 19: Comment on Jeremiah 10:12, 13; *Institutes*, I, v, 9; II, ii, 13ff.

[53] *Institutes*, II, ii, 12ff.; Comment on Jno. 4:36; Dowey, *op. cit.*, p. 139f.; Krusche, *op. cit.*, p. 104.

[54] *Institutes*, II, ii, 15.

[55] *Ibid.*, II, ii, 12. If we say, according to Calvin, that the unbeliever cannot know anything "we not only go against God's Word, but also run contrary to the experience of common sense."

[56] Zanche, *De Operibus*, Epistle Dedicatory, had this to say: "There is nothing more noble, nothing more in accordance with the dignity of man, including Christians, nothing which gives more solid pleasure, nothing more useful and therefore by the theologian to be least neglected but rather most accurately studied, than the attentive and diligent contemplation of the works established by God." Cf. Pt. I, Lib. I, cap. i; Pt. II, Lib. IV, cap. iv. His position on creation and providence obviously prevented him from holding to a thorough Aristotelianism.

properly guided would lead to the truth.[57] The clearest statement of the Calvinistic position, however, comes from Francis Bacon:

> To conclude therefore, let no man upon a weak conceit of sobriety or an ill-applied moderation think or maintain that a man can search too far, or be too well studied in the book of God's word or in the book of God's works—divinity or philosophy: but rather let men endeavour an endless progress and proficiency in both; only let them beware that they apply both to charity, and not to swelling; to use not to ostentation; and again that they do not unwisely mingle or confound these learnings together.[58]

This naturally brings one face to face with the question of the statements of the Scriptures concerning natural phenomena and happenings. Is the Bible the final authority on matters scientific? To this Calvin replied that when the Spirit of God speaks through the Law and the Prophets he does so not with rigorous exactness, "but in a style suited to the common capacities of man."[59] This of course would not involve the question of miracles, for they are special occurrences for some particular purpose, but for the knowledge of all normal natural happenings the study of the phenomena, not of the Scriptures, brings man true knowledge.[60] Of this point of view one finds many echoes in most Calvinistic writings down into the seventeenth century.[61]

---

[57] Hooykaas, *op. cit.*, p. 186. Ramus, it would seem, did not feel that sin had corrupted man's "natural reason" so that he could not think without divine grace. In this he did not go as far as his fellow Calvinists who believed that the Fall wrecked man's thinking capacity to the extent that he needed divine assistance for a true understanding of nature.

[58] *Advancement*, p. 8. Cf. also pp. 88ff., 186.

[59] In his comment on Ps. 19:4, Calvin points out that David "accommodating himself to the rudest and dullest . . . confines himself to the ordinary appearances of the eye. . . ." Comment on Jer. 1:12, 13; Torrance, *op. cit.*, p. 45; Dillenberger, *op. cit.*, pp. 32ff.

[60] Comment on Genesis 1:16.

[61] Zanche, *De Operibus*, Pt. III, Lib. I, cap. i; Waddington, *op. cit.*, pp. 359f.; Dillenberger, *op. cit.*, p. 61.

Such an attitude to the Bible and nature meant that Calvin and his followers flatly rejected any form of biblicistic rationalism or mysticism. As Calvin put it, "He who would learn astronomy and other recondite arts, let him go elsewhere."[62] This anti-rationalist approach lay at the basis of his rejection of judicial astrology. Similarly, Ramus and Bacon spent considerable time blasting at astrology, alchemy, and the esoteric philosophy of Paracelsus who attempted to deduce all scientific truth by means of rationalization from the Scriptures, and declared all other knowledge of nature false. Even philosophical rationalism came under attack. Ramus and Bacon flatly rejected the deductive-syllogistic method as inadequate for science, since it dealt with notions rather than with facts of nature,[63] while Palissy and Paré defended their practices on grounds of experience alone.[64]

It is through the facts of nature that one learns about nature. In his tractate on astrology and in his pamphlet advocating the creation of an inventory of all religious relics in Europe, [65] Calvin continually pointed to the need for ascertaining the facts, even as in a theological argument he continually went back to what the Bible said. "Je ne veux rejetter l'art qui est tiré de l'ordre de nature, mais que je le prise et loue comme un don singulier de Dieu."[66] This in turn became the central theme of Calvin's "scientific" disciples. Ramus made a considerable reputation for himself by rejecting every "hypothesis"

---

[62] Comment on Gen. 1:6.

[63] Hooykaas, *op. cit.*, pp. 218, 247, 274f., 278f.; Bacon, *Advancement*, pp. 100, 216ff. and Aphorism XXIII *Novum Organum*, *Works*, V, 51: "There is a great difference between the Idols of the human mind and the Ideas of the divine. That is to say between certain empty dogmas, and the true signatures and marks set upon the works of creation as they are found in nature."

[64] Morley, *op. cit.*, II, 101; Ambrose Paré, "Apology and Treatise," in F. R. Packard, *op. cit.*, pp. 129ff.

[65] "An admonition showing the advantage which Christendom might derive from an Inventory of Relics," *Tracts Relating to the Reformation*, ed., H. Beveridge (Edinburgh, 1860), I, 255.

[66] "Advertissement," Coll. 529.

which did not keep strictly to the facts.[67] Palissy attacked Paracelsus, Raymond Lull and the alchemists on the same grounds, preparing a cabinet of geological specimens to support his case.[68] And again Bacon sums up the whole matter in his preface to the *Novum Organum* when he expresses the hope that he has brought about the marriage of "the empirical and rational faculties," in order that God may enable him to present further gifts to the family of men.[69]

This emphasis upon the factual and empirical raises an important question. How did they propose to find the "fact"? In the development which took place between 1570 and 1620 one sees a change in the answers offered. The earlier and more humanistically inclined writers such as Zanche and Ramus thought not in terms of experimentation, but in terms of the statements of ancient authorities: Aristotle's *Meteors,* Pliny's *Natural History* and the like.[70] With Palissy who prided himself on knowing no Latin or Greek, and with Paré the military surgeon, practical experience predominated. They found their facts through rudimentary experimentation, whether in the firing of pottery vessels or in the testing out of

---

[67] Hooykaas, *op. cit.*, pp. 178ff., 183ff., 269; Waddington, *op. cit.*, p. 355.

[68] *Oeuvres*, pp. 394ff.; Morley, *op. cit.*, II, 101; J. Huizinga, *Men and Ideas* (New York, 1959), p. 304.

[69] *Novum Organum, Works,* IV, 19.

[70] Zanche, *De Operibus, passim* continually quotes the ancients as authorities who record what they saw happening. In this he revealed clearly the influence of the Renaissance humanistic method. (Gilbert, *op. cit.*, p. 110.) W. J. Ong, *op. cit.*, p. 268, seems to fail to understand that Ramus in following the same method felt that he was being truly empirical. True, he did not perform experiments himself, but, under the influence of contemporary humanism, he believed that he could trust Aristotle's observations completely, despite his repeated and vigorous rejection of the Philosopher's theories. As Hooykaas, *op. cit.*, pp. 199ff., has pointed out, while Ramus felt that experimentation was beneath a scholar's dignity he stressed the importance of the careful observation and measurement of phenomena. In this sense he helped to lay the groundwork for experimental investigation.

new methods of tying up wounds.[71] By the time Bacon wrote, under the influence of such men as Ramus and Palissy, experimentation albeit of a somewhat haphazard type had begun to become the principal means of "invention and discovery" in the study of nature.[72]

Then came the problem of the way in which the facts discovered should be treated or as they said "judged." Calvin, while stressing the importance of facts, had said little on this subject, but he had in his biblical-theological studies developed a method. One might call it the method of logical arrangement and relationship, by which he placed his biblical material in certain theological loci or topics set in an order of progression. For instance, he began his *Institutes of the Christian Religion* with the doctrine of the knowledge of God and ended with a discussion of the outward form of the church and the nature of civil government. In this he seems to have thought primarily of a teaching technique which led in logical fashion from knowledge to action. In matters relating to physical science, however, although he spoke in terms of natural law and natural order, he never developed any specific pattern of method.

Consequently, one finds that "method" developed only very gradually. Zanche worked out a kind of Protestant scholasticism, but this satisfied few.[73] Most of those in the Calvinistic stream of thought sought a single method which would do away with Aristotle completely and which would produce results firmly based upon facts

[71] Palissey has caused considerable discussion since his nineteenth-century biographers, such as Morley, *op. cit.*, pp. 26ff, and Dumesnil, *op. cit.*, p. 19, hold that he employed a truly empirical method while a later writer, such as H. Brown, *op. cit.*, p. 35, maintains that his whole method was "hit and miss." Perhaps Huizinga's interpretation lies nearest the truth when he states that Palissy's "place is among those minds who enthusiastically hunted and grubbed in nature to discover its secrets and thus prepared the way for a positivistic natural science" (*op. cit.*, p. 304). Paré obviously followed the same pattern of thought and action. Packard, *op. cit.*, pp. 129ff.

[72] Bacon, *Advancement*, pp. 122ff.; Huizinga, *op. cit.*, p. 304.

[73] Gilbert, *op. cit.*, pp. 110.

alone. In this attempt Peter Ramus took a major share, for he taught that the arts arise out of the facts. Man's natural reason takes the facts, sorts them according to their natural order into groups, loci or topics, and gradually combining them eventually produces general principles or precepts. Thus he does not begin with hypotheses but with the facts, allowing them to lead him naturally to certain conclusions.[74] Bacon, accepting a good part of this, carried the matter farther by insisting that such examination or judgment should lead on to the discovery of new facts and new relationships. This he termed "magistral" judgment.[75] Thus, as W. J. Ong has pointed out, the method was based on the idea of space and arrangement which themselves were part of nature, a method very closely linked to that of the theologian and his *loci theologici.*[76]

The influence of the theologian and his teaching methods appears even more clearly when one examines what Bacon calls "the method of tradition" or exposition. From Calvin down to Bacon the primary purpose of the scholar was that of teaching. All Calvin's writings show this and those who followed him in the scientific field have the same approach.[77] Palissy wrote and collected his geological specimens for this purpose[78] and Ramus

---

[74] Hooykaas, *op. cit.*, pp. 188ff., 218ff., points out that Ramus insisted upon beginning with the facts in any attempt to build up a science, although he stressed the necessity of commencing from the most general principles in teaching. Cf. Gilbert, *op. cit.*, p. 1.

[75] Bacon, *op. cit.*, pp. 93ff.; Boas, *op. cit.*, pp. 250ff.

[76] Ong, in his criticism of Ramus, seems to have overlooked the fact that the "geometrical" method was regarded by many as the most "natural," and this method in a sense was that of the typical logic of the theologians. *Op. cit.*, pp. 196f., 288, 354f.; Gilbert, *op. cit.*, pp. 84ff.

[77] Cf. the full title of Calvin's major work, *Christianae Religionis Institutio Totam Fere Pietatis Summam et Quiquid est in Doctrina Salutis Cognitu Necessarium Complectens Omnibus Pietatis Studiosis Lectu Dignissimum Opus ac Recens Editum.* Cf. H. Obendiek, "Die Institutio Calvins als 'Confessio' und 'Apologie,'" *Theologische Aufsätze,* Karl Barth zum 50 Geburstag, ed., M. Lempp and E. Wolf (Munich, 1936), pp. 418ff.

[78] Dumesnil, *op. cit.*, pp. 24ff.; Morley, *op. cit.*, pp. 102f.; Palissy, *Oeuvres*, pp. 434ff.

thought much more of a "teaching" than a "research" method. The latter usually came in only as an afterthought. This would seem to be the reason for Ramus' reputation as a man who mixed rhetoric and dialectic, although in point of fact the rhetorical aspect of his method formed only a small part of his whole system.[79] It remained for Francis Bacon to distinguish clearly between the two types of method and to insist that they should not be confused.[80] Yet in their teaching or rhetorical methods both Ramus and Bacon insisted fervently that everything must find its basis in solid facts as one moves from the better known to the less known. Even in this, however, the topical order was to govern as one set forth one's ideas as convincingly as possible.[81]

At this point one feels obliged to ask whether mathematics played any part in this concept of method. As far as one can tell, Calvin, Zanche, Beza and the others had little interest in such matters. Francis Bacon went even further, expressing a fear of the subject since he felt that the mathematician always tended to over-simplify for the benefit of a neat numerical scheme. This provided part of the reason for his doubts concerning Copernicus.[82] Ramus, on the other hand, from the time of his open conversion to Protestantism increasingly stressed the need for mathematical studies and their application to the science of nature. Seeing that he had little or no interest in actual experimentation, this may appear strange, but if one remembers that his basic method was one of arrangement in space, one can understand perhaps why geometry and arithmetic played such

[79] Ong, *op. cit.*, pp. 283f.; Gilbert, *op. cit.*, pp. 136, 221; Hooykaas, *op. cit.*, pp. 222ff.

[80] *Advancement*, p. 140.

[81] *Ibid.*, pp. 141ff.; Hooykaas, *op. cit.*, pp. 195f.; Gilbert, *op. cit.*, pp. 134-143.

[82] *Advancement*, pp. 98f., 129ff.; *Novum Organum*, pp. 47ff.; S. F. Mason, *A History of the Sciences* (London, 1953), p. 114.

an important part in his scheme of things.[83] Thus in Calvinistic thought relating to nature and natural phenomena, although the stress still lay on the qualitative rather than on the quantitative, the tendency to regard the geometrical arranging of the facts as the truly "scientific" method became increasingly prominent. In this way mathematics almost imperceptibly entered the picture.

Although mathematics obtained no great recognition, Calvinistic thinking concerning nature possessed another characteristic still very important: a stress upon objectivity. Calvin held that God had objectified his revelation in the Scriptures and in nature, so that man could comprehend both by a proper analysis in the light of eternity. This forced him to avoid speculation in order that he might truly hear God speaking. He rejected any idea of a creative tradition and of a concept of dialogue with the world. Man's dialogue is with God.[84] The realism of Palissy's "rustic pieces" and Ramus' stress upon the study of nature external to man along with his insistence that rhetoric involved only ornament and delivery while reason dealt with the understanding of the facts, both came out of this tradition. Ramus clearly feared, as Ong has said, "the obtrusion of voices and persons in scientific issues."[85] This same attitude ap-

---

[83] Although Melanchthon and Agricola both favored the study of mathematics, they never attempted to apply it universally. John Sturm of Strasburg did to a certain extent, and through his influence Ramus sought to apply it to the quadrivium of the medieval curriculum. His interest in physical science and in particular in mathematics seems to have arisen at the time of his conversion to Protestantism, a point which Waddington, Hooykaas and Ong all miss. Ramus left an endowment for the establishment of a chair of mathematics in the Université de France. Waddington, *op. cit.*, pp. 246ff.; Hooykaas, *op. cit.*, pp. 196-251; Ong, *op. cit.*, pp. 30ff., 196 f., Gilbert, *op. cit.*, pp. 84ff.

[84] *Institutes*, I, v, 5. "We must therefore admit in God's individual works—but especially in them as a whole—that God's powers actually appear as in a painting" (I, v, 10). Cf. Torrance, *op. cit.*, p. 44.

[85] Ong, *op. cit.*, pp. 287ff.; Waddington, *op. cit.*, p. 346; Hooykaas, *op. cit.*, pp. 183f., 221.

pears in Bacon when he speaks of God framing "the mind of man as a mirror or glass, capable of the image of the universal world, and joyful to receive the impression thereof, as the eye joyeth to receive light. . . ."[86] Without bias caused by rhetoric, therefore, man should seek to know and to interpret nature. Objective investigation alone could adequately set forth the truth.

The ultimate goal of all scientific method is the establishment of the most general principles by establishing an all-inclusive system. So thought Calvin, whether dealing with matters theological or matters physical, and his successors felt much the same way.[87] And yet they also admitted that both in theology and in natural science there always remains for man an ultimate surd which man cannot break down for analysis. This does not result from some obduracy of nature, but rather from the mystery of God the creator and upholder of all things. One must seek as far as possible to discover the system in the universe by empirical means, but at the same time must acknowledge that some parts will always remain unknown. In this way and by these means the Calvinists endeavored to provide an understanding of nature which would supplant that of Aristotle.

The Use of Nature

One cannot speak about the Calvinistic concept of nature and of scientific method without at least referring to one other important facet of thought. Neither Calvin nor those who came after him held any brief for mere learning as such. Man's knowledge and abilities must be applied to use. This idea was by no means Calvin's

---

[86] *Advancement*, p. 5. Cf. also pp. 23f., 121, 129ff., 141, 146.

[87] Calvin, *Institutes*, I, v, 5, 11, 12; Zanche, *De Operibus*, Epistle Dedicatory; Hooykaas *op. cit.*, p. 240; Bacon, *Novum Organum*, pp. 47ff.; *Advancement*, pp. 5, 95ff., 215; Haydn, *op. cit.*, pp. 267ff.; Hall, *op. cit.*, p. xvi.

invention, but it fitted in well with his point of view and received support from those who followed him.[88]

Calvin held on biblical-theological grounds that God had placed man upon this earth to subdue and use it. Thus man should employ the good gifts of God for his own physical and emotional well-being.[89] This utilitarian approach one finds in the others who have been mentioned as following in his footsteps: Zanche, Palissy, Paré, Ramus and Bacon as well as many others.[90] But the highest end of all scientific, as well as theological, studies is ultimately the glory of God. As all of creation is the handiwork of God, the study, the analysis and synthesis of it, and the explanation of its wonders, all have as their ultimate end and purpose the manifestation and revelation of the infinite wisdom, power and grace of the Triune Godhead.[91]

How much influence did the Calvinistic school of thought exercise? It would seem that in some areas—France, Holland, Western Germany, England and Scotland—it gained a very considerable following. Calvin's writings themselves were widespread, laying the foundation for this point of view.[92] The works of Ramus, also translated into many different languages, made their impress in various places. The English Puritans and the Scottish Presbyterians, for instance, accepted most of his ideas with the result that Gresham College in England,

---

[88] Bohatec, *op. cit.*, pp. 263; Gilbert, *op. cit.*, pp. 69f.; Hooykaas, *op. cit.*, pp. 187ff.; Ong. *op. cit.*, pp. 224f.

[89] Comment on 1 Cor. 1:17; Bohatec, *op. cit.*, pp. 263; Nash, *op. cit.*, pp. 67f.

[90] Zanche, *op. cit.*, pp. 329ff.; Hooykaas, *op. cit.*, pp. 222ff.; Palissy, *op. cit.*, pp. 231ff.

[91] Calvin in his attack on Astrology states the Reformed position most clearly: "Surquoi je dis brièvement, que nulle bonne science n'est répugnante à la crainte de Dieu mis à la doctrine qu'il nous donne pour nous mêner en la vie eternelle, moyennant que nous ne mettions la charrue devant les boeufs: c'est à dire que nous ayens cette prudence de nous servit des arts tant liberaux que méchaniques en passant par ce monde, pour tendre toujours au Royaume céleste" (*Advertissement*, p. 540f). Zanche, *De Operibus*, Epistle Dedicatory; Bacon, *Advancement*, pp. 7, 36.

[92] Lecerf, *op. cit.*, p. 118.

Edinburgh University in Scotland and Harvard College in Massachusetts all began their existences primarily as Ramist institutions. Added to this Ramus received much attention in the Netherlands and Germany.[93] Similarly Bacon had his adherents not only in England but also on the Continent. Thus, the Calvinistic schools of thought exercised an important influence on the development of scientific thought in the sixteenth century.

Yet one must recognize that the Calvinistic tradition had its serious weaknesses. Its interest more in teaching than in experimental research, its failure to use mathematics, and its continued thinking in qualitative rather than quantitative terms concerning natural phenomena show this. Furthermore, because of these deficiencies it never really devised an effective method of research. Consequently, it did not directly force a scientific advance.

Despite these limitations, however, it played an important part in the breaking down of the old scientific order. It undermined the medieval synthesis at every level with its stress upon the factual and its insistence on objective analysis of phenomena in order that all things might be subordinated to law and formed into a system. Moreover, the use of a "special" method, instead of a search for purpose and final causes in nature, helped to give a new view of nature so that men began to ask different questions of nature with startling results.[94]

Thus Calvinism's influence, while not leading necessarily to the scientific revolution, was one of the important movements which helped to prepare the way for seventeenth-century developments in the work of such men as Kepler, van Huygens and Newton, and provides us today with an integration of religion and science in the ultimate Christian theistic environment of all created reality.

---

[93] Kristeller, *op. cit.*, p. 43; Hooykaas, *op. cit.*, pp. 279f.

[94] Crombie, *Augustine to Galileo*, pp. 274f.; Hooykaas, *op. cit.*, pp. 288ff.; Ong, *op. cit.*, p. 268; Burtt, *op. cit.*, pp. 27ff.

CHAPTER IV

THE CONTEMPORARY CHALLENGE TO CHRISTIAN SCHOLARSHIP

Dietrich Bonhoeffer, a Luthern minister executed by the Nazis at the close of World War II, wrote to a friend during his imprisonment that the world had now entered a non-religious era, from which man had banished God completely. All man's recent achievements in science, art and other fields, Bonhoeffer felt, he has brought about without any reference to God. Consequently, to speak to modern man of God is to speak of the irrelevant. Man, in his present situation, feels no need for God, for, although he may not conceive of himself as self-sufficient, he believes that he must make his decisions solely with reference to his own situation, so that even if God does exist he possesses no vital importance.[1]

As one looks at the present state of, not only Western, but also world, thought, one might say that Bonhoeffer's generalization possesses even more validity now than it did twenty years ago. And the field in which this point of view seems to be most common is that of scholarship. The average Christian going about his daily work in the office, the farm or the home may not directly encounter this attitude, although no doubt it is always present. The scholar, on the other hand, having to deal with precise problems of the interpretation of the facts of the universe finds that this challenge faces him at all times. To think as a Christian when dealing with the sciences or arts, requires that he must ready himself to oppose the idea that Christianity is irrelevant to modern thought. Here is the challenge to which he must reply.

---

[1] *Letters and Papers from Prison,* London (Fontana) 1959, pp. 90ff. Cf. the same idea as expressed from the other side in Julian Huxley, "A Biologist looks at Man," *Fortune,* XXVI (1942), 139ff.

A Challenge Implies a Denial of Validity

When one throws down a challenge to another's position or point of view, the challenger by implication declares that his opponent is wrong and that his position fails to measure up to certain standards. Such is the essence of the non-Christian challenge to Christian scholarship. To the non-Christian scholar Christian scholarship cannot rise to the requirements of "scientific standards," whatever those standards may be.

In order to see, however, the nature of this disagreement one must first of all understand the term "Christian scholarship," and wherein it differs from "secular scholarship." Otherwise, one will find oneself talking in a vacuum.

To clarify this difference, one must first ask the question: Is Christian scholarship merely theological, or does it cover a larger area? Does it, or should it, deal with the fields of history, philosophy, natural science and the like? Some Christians seem to think of scholarship only in terms of theology, while others will extend the area somewhat more widely. What then is the field of Christian scholarship? Does it differ from that of non-Christian scholarship?

To begin with, Christianity itself makes the widest possible claims. When one becomes a Christian "all things become new" (2 Cor. 5:17). Christian scholarship can never limit itself to a narrow field of biblical studies or theological discussion. Rather it claims that the whole of creation belongs to God and to his Christ. Consequently, Christian scholarship cannot but deal with every facet of creation, whether biology, history, medicine, politics, fine arts or any other field which one may name. Christian scholarship claims as its parish, the universe. The only difficulty is that many Christians fail to see the fullness of its scope.

True Christian scholarship, however, is not merely wide; it is also deep. It should never content itself with brushing or scratching the surface. It must delve to the very depths of all God's creation. This means hard work, thorough, penetrating thought and effort in order that the Christian scholar may dig deep in his "unfathomable mine" to know the truth. It means wrestling with problems, not merely glancing over them, and it also means exactitude and care in everything the scholar does. Only too frequently Christian scholarship has been slipshod and facile, whereas it should show itself exhaustive and even exhausting. Here we have our ideal, but who may attain unto it?

Yet in saying this we have not demonstrated that the scholarship of which we have spoken manifests any peculiar Christian traits. Secular scholarship shows itself to be just as universal and just as exhaustive. The Christian scholar, however, must hold that such characteristics have value only when the scholar carries on his work in the light of the divinely revealed Word of the Old and New Testaments. All his effort and work amount to something only when he does his work continually in the light of the triune God as creator, sustainer and redeemer. Enlightened by the Holy Spirit speaking through the Scriptures, he looks at this world, seeing in it the handiwork of the sovereign God.[2]

Nevertheless, the Christian scholar may never lay claim to final or ultimate knowledge of this world. God who sustains, rules and redeems us may never be brought down to or contained in, the little temples of men's scholarly systems—even Christian systems. Here men see only through a glass darkly, so that although one be ever so careful in his study of the Scriptures and of the created world, he cannot possibly relate the two absolutely and all along the line. Where God has clarified the relationship between time and eternity one may see and understand a little, but where he has left darkness

[2] John Calvin, *Institutes of the Christian Religion*, bk. I, chaps. VI, VII; C. Van Til, *The Defence of the Faith*, Philadelphia, 1955, pp. 60ff.

there the Christian scholar must pause, even come to a dead stop. He must continually realize that God has placed limitations to his knowledge and to his understanding, of God himself and of his work in time. Thus, although new knowledge continually comes forth from both the Word and creation, no man, even the greatest Christian scholar, can say: "I have said the last word."[3]

While recognizing the limitations of his knowledge, the Christian scholar claims that only in the light of God's self-revelation can one obtain a true knowledge of his creation. At this point many may object that a large part of the scientists who have accomplished great things in the past half century have made no claim to any belief in God. Would the Christian claim that they have not truly been scientists? To this the Christian must reply that he gladly recognizes all that the non-Christian has accomplished, but at the same time he believes two things. First, the non-Christian has gained his knowledge by the grace of God; and secondly, the non-Christian does not really understand the significance of his own achievements. Only in the light of eternity can any man do this, so that when one commences by denying eternity's existence or significance, one never attains to what might be termed an ultimate view. Only the Christian scholar sees his work and his results in their proper context, their proper environment, that of the eternal God.

The Christian scholar believes this because he holds that in order to know and understand the things of the universe, one must think analogically to the thinking of God; he must think God's thoughts after him. Thus whether he studies the stars, the molecules, fungi or the rise and fall of kingdoms, the Christian in truth seeks to know these things that he may also know him who is the sovereign over all. Moreover, he endeavors to have this light on all his work, that he may ever have a true per-

[3] Cf. Calvin, *ibid.*, I, XVII, 2.

spective upon his work, and so obtain knowledge which, although limited, is true as far as it goes.[4]

The Christian would go even farther than this, however, for he would hold that only by predicating an ultimately personal and rational background to the whole of the universe can one believe in any form of scholarship. If this universe has no meaning, has no rationale, being simply a collection of unconnected atoms banging around in space-time, scholarship must end before it starts. Only Christianity and the Christian picture of our universe makes scholarship possible, for only on that basis can the scholar speak of any form of continuity in the universe either in time or space. Without Christianity and the Christian interpretation, scholarship simply could not exist, for rationality even on the part of the scholar would disappear.

At the same time no Christian could grant that one may come to a knowledge of God, simply through the logical necessity of accepting a Christian philosophy which makes sense out of the universe. A man, whether scholar or not, will come to the Christian position only by the grace of God working in him through the Holy Spirit. Only when one becomes "a new creature" may one then "see all things new." Not by logic, reason or the scientific method does one arrive at a true interpretation, but only by the action of God who has redeemed him in Christ and regenerated him through the Holy Spirit.[5]

To this whole position the non-Christian returns a firm and oft-repeated "nyet." He thinks the Christian position silly and ridiculous, for it makes God, not man, the center of the universe. Man pleases himself with the idea that he stands in the central point of all things, at least intellectually. He is normal, i.e., he has no particular malfunction of the mind or understanding, and he is auton-

---

[4] A. Lecerf, *Etudes Calvinistes*, Paris, 1949, pp. 115f.

[5] A. Kuyper, *The Work of the Holy Spirit*, New York, 1908, p. 310; R. Niebuhr, "A Faith for History's Greatest Crisis," *Fortune*, XXVI (1942), 99f.

omous, i.e., free and independent in both thought and action.[6] Moreover by means of the scientific method he has succeeded in discovering many of the secrets of the universe without any reference to God. Consequently, he does not need to bother with him. As Titov, one of the Russian spacemen, commented after his orbit around the earth, "I did not see any sign of God." Thus the modern humanist regards all this Christian talk about God, creation, etc., as irrelevant. Man is sufficient unto himself.

At this point some may object that when we look at the picture of scholarship today, we find that many scholars are far from being atheists. Indeed, in Russia the scientists' growing belief that the universe has behind it ultimately a spiritual reality has caused much worry in Communist Party circles. Similarly in the Western world a tradition has grown up as the result of the writings of such men as Max Planck, Lecomte du Nouy and others that behind all, one must conclude that a god exists.[7] While this is true, this God is hardly the God and Father of our Lord Jesus Christ. Usually limited by man and by the creation in which man lives, unable to do very much, he is rather ineffective. Indeed he remains a sort of mystery about which man knows little or nothing since he seems to have little or no relationship to the universe which the scholar studies. In a sense, he remains almost as irrelevant as the "god" of the thoroughgoing agnostic or atheist.[8]

Moreover, whether one holds to a completely humanistic position or accepts the idea of a limited mystery known as "god," usually the result is a denial of the claims of Christian scholarship. For one thing, the

---

[6] This point of view shows itself repeatedly in many contemporary works such as Bertrand Russell's *Mysticism and Logic* or W. MacNeile Dixon's *The Human Situation.*

[7] M. Planck, *Scientific Autobiography and Other Papers,* tr. F. Gaynor, New York, 1949, pp. 155ff, 174ff.; P. Lecomte du Nouy, *Human Destiny,* New York, 1947, chap. 16.

[8] Cf. A. W. Munk, *History and God,* New York, 1952, chaps. 5, 8, who expresses the common view of those who hold this position.

non-Christian objects because the Christian comes to his work with certain presupposition. He is not neutral. He has, therefore, prepared a case, even before his study has commenced. This the non-Christian cannot accept, even though he in turn comes with presuppositions which say that Christianity is wrong and he can logically and properly be neutral. He believes his position to be correct, while denying that the Christian has any right to say that he takes seriously the fact of the sovereign triune God.

Thus Christian scholarship always rests under a cloud as far as the non-Christian is concerned. Even among the most polite, one repeatedly discovers an attitude of contempt. "How can a man be a scholar and a Christian at the same time. The two things are incompatible." Here then is the first facet of the contemporary challenge to Christian scholarship—a denial of its validity not only as truth but even as a system of thought which one must seriously consider.

A Challenge Asserts a Claim to Superiority

Modern man asserts without any hesitation that he is superior to all the generations which have gone before by virtue of his knowledge and use of the scientific approach. Has he not accomplished things considered before this generation as the dreams of romancers? Jules Verne's *Around the World in Eighty Days* has nothing to offer in competition to the orbiting of a Gagarin, a Shepard, a Titov or a Glenn. By his own brains and scientific know-how he has succeeded in doing unbelievable things without any reference to a god. Man is superior to any need of God—or so he thinks. Thus the contemporary scientific humanist negatively denies the validity of the Christian position, while he positively asserts the sole authority of his approach and method.

He grounds the assertion of his superiority upon the results he has attained, but he goes even farther. He believes that he has formulated a method which provides a logical and rational approach to all problems. He has, moreover, discovered by means of the scientific method a way of dealing with the hard, cold brute facts of the universe, so that he now can examine, analyze and synthesize them into a scientific pattern or structure which enables him to understand and manipulate them. He feels quite confident that this method applied to every aspect of life and human activity will bring assured scientific results. One physical scientist has even set himself up as one who by the use of his techniques can bring universal peace. The scientific method without God holds the solution to all questions.

Yet despite all his assurance that the "neutral" scientific approach satisfies all problems, man always seems to have lurking at the back of his mind a gnawing doubt. Despite all the research and experimentation performed in physiology, psychology, sociology and similar disciplines man still has not even approached perfection. Added to this, having banished God from the universe and replaced him with Chance, man faces a hostile or at best a completely indifferent environment, a belief which cannot but lead to despair. Lord Russell in his essay "A Free Man's Worship," asserts that only such "invincible despair" can fortify one's heart and mind to face life.[9]

The Christian only too often when faced with this philosophy of life tends to give in to it. He may even at times mistakingly think that such an outlook has a fundamentally Christian orientation. But if he really holds to a Christian position he cannot possibly submit. The refrain "Science is truth, truth science; that's all you know and all you need to know," he simply cannot accept. If he takes seriously the Christian doctrine of God as creator, sustainer and redeemer, he cannot possibly agree that the humanistic scientific position is superior or even equal to that of the Christian's interpretation. Nor may

[9] Russell, *op. cit.*, London, 1953, chap. III.

he even consider for an instant that despair provides the ultimate refuge for man. He believes that only in the light of God's eternity, can man obtain a true understanding of this universe in which he lives.[10]

At the same time, however, the Christian cannot but acknowledge that the unbeliever who employes the scientific method without any reference to ultimate things does achieve great success. Julian Huxley declared that the accomplishments of modern science and scholarship have freed man from the need for any ideas of a god, and many echo his sentiments.[11] The Christian, on the other hand, believes that the worshiper of science achieves his success only by the goodness of God who has restrained the effect of sin upon man's mind. He has endowed men with great gifts which he enables them to employ in interpreting and exploiting this world. Yet this does not lead men to an acknowledgement of the Truth in its ultimate character as God himself. Instead men prefer to say that chance is ultimate, and by so doing they show that even their scientific achievements have at their very base a logical contradiction. They may achieve much in a relatively limited sphere, but they do so despite, not because of, their basic philosophy.[12]

The reason for the Christian holding this interpretation rests on the fact that no one can think or act without making certain assumptions concerning the ultimate character of reality. Even Julian Huxley's pontifical statements do not eliminate this necessity. When a scholar engages in his research and analysis he assumes either an ultimate chance or an ultimate rationality, and he then proceeds to reason toward either of these goals. In this way his assumption, in the final decision, determines his conclusion, although he may fail to realize this. Indeed he may ostensibly assume a

---

[10] I Corinthians, chaps. 1, 2.

[11] Huxley, *op. cit.*, p. 152.

[12] Cf. C. Van Til, *Common Grace*, Philadelphia, 1947, pp. 3f.

basically irrational universe, while in truth he takes it for granted that both he and his environment have rational structures. Thus one's true assumptions are of the greatest importance, particularly when one deals with this matter of the non-Christian's sense of superiority.

But let us look a little more closely at these presuppositions. If the universe is ultimately rational, one may perhaps adopt the view of complete and absolute determinism. The universe then becomes a great monstrous machine in which human personality, decision and action lose their significance since they become merely unintelligent cogs driven by impersonal forces. But if this be the case, one must raise the question of the validity of human thought and interpretation along with that of the origin of this "rationally" structured universe. Did it come by accident, or by the design of a creator? If originated through the work of a Creator only the Christian-theistic doctrine makes sense of either man or his environment. If no Creator acted, then chance alone is the ultimate source of rationality.

If one prefers chance to a personal Creator, as do such thinkers as Russell and Jeans,[13] one must then answer another question: Whence comes rationality—the rationality of the scholar and the rationality of the universe? If both the subject and object of knowledge are irrational how can one possibly devise a structure known as empirical science? Indeed, how can two scholars communicate to each other the chance phantasmagoria of their own minds? Even an admission that there may be a limited God who partially controls things does not answer the question since he also must depend upon chance, particularly for the understanding of himself. Here lies the weakness of the theological position of a Toynbee.[14] If

---

[13] Sir James Jeans, *The Mysterious Universe*, Cambridge, 1944, chap. I.

[14] A. Toynbee, *An Historian's Approach to Religion*, Oxford, 1956, chaps. 19, 20.

one admits chance in one place in the universe, one must always assume that chance is involved everywhere, an interpretation fatal to science and scholarship. Even the production and continuance of limited rationality by chance is itself irrational.

The only satisfactory basis for scholarship would then seem to be that proposed by the Christian, for only on the basis of biblical teaching concerning the personality, the sovereignty, the creative, sustaining, and redeeming activity of the triune God alone can one presuppose for scholarship a knowable universe. The non-Christian in employing the scientific method contravenes his own rules for he assumes the universe to have a structure possible only on Christian grounds. He rejects Christianity as invalid, claims his humanistic empiricism to be superior to the Christian interpretation, and yet quite openly builds his scholarly edifice upon a foundation proper to none but Christian thought. Thus, despite his denials of Christianity he adopts the Christian starting point in order to produce illogically a system which he holds to be immeasurably superior to the Christian system.

The unbeliever very often excels the Christian as both scientist and scholar, but he does so not because he is "neutral" with regard to the ultimate meaning of the universe. He has in fact stolen from the Christian his interpretation in order that he might establish a doctrine to the glory of man. As long as he remains within the confines of the physical and human realm this does not appear so clearly, but once he begins to speak of ultimate problems, his inconsistency and his weakness immediately appear. He claims superiority to the Christian position but in the final analysis, he depends upon it even for his most mundane thoughts and activities.

That the non-Christian's claims are sweeping none can deny. Asserting that the Christian approach is invalid, he claims that his position alone offers a proper explanation of the phenomenal world. At this point many Christians begin to back away from the whole question, since they feel inadequate to meet such claims head-on. When Christian students enroll in college or university, they frequently tend to avoid courses which they feel might raise questions concerning their faith. Others will not do research in topics which do not relate specifically to religious or Christian matters. It often looks as though the Christian fears that perhaps the humanistic scientist may be right after all.

Is this the position which the Christian should take? To this the answer would seem to be a definite no. He must place himself directly in front of the non-Christian challenge and stand up to it as part of his Christian testimony. Far too many Christians adopt the attitude that personal testimony consists in a plea with some individual to accept Christ as Savior, and they forget that today Christian scholarship also provides a very important means of Christian testimony. A prayer meeting does not constitute an adequate reply to non-Christian scientific scepticism, for it does not answer the questions in relevant terms. Christians must reply to the contemporary challenge in terms of scholarship.

To this end God has called some specifically to the field of scholarship. For a long time most Christians regarded those who went into scholarship as a life occupation as seeking an avenue of escape from the ministry. But today this attitude in some quarters is changing, and an increasing number of Christians are turning to the fields of education and research. They must, however, continually remember that the call to scholarship is a divine call as much as is a call to the ministry or to the mission field. Furthermore, only as one considers it as a call will one fulfill one's obligations adequately, for the work of a scholar may become extremely dull and boring unless one has a deep-rooted sense of vocation.

And this call comes not merely to work in the biblical and theological fields. Most Christians will admit that in dealing with the problems of textual criticism, biblical and systematic theology, apologetics, practical theology and church history, Christian scholarship must vindicate its position. They forget, only too frequently, however, that every thought and every interpretation must come under the rule of Jesus Christ, that all facts whether of biology, astronomy, history, economics or literature must be looked at in the light of eternity. Consequently, Christian scholarship must manifest itself in every field by showing that no matter where one starts in the universe, every fact receives a proper interpretation only in the light of biblical teaching, and that only when one looks at the universe in the light of divine creation, providence and redemption does it make any sense, so making scholarship possible.

This of course means that the Christian scholar must be a dedicated man: because of his dedication to Christ, dedicated also to his scholarly pursuits. Sloppy work, short cuts and the like should have no place in his program. Unfortunately, only too frequently Christian undergraduates apparently feel that since going to college has one sole purpose, that of providing them with a job, they do not need to work hard. They do not seem to grasp the fact that their college years are those in which they should grow greatly in their understanding of the works of the sovereign God, and that they can grow only by hard work. They must, as all Christian scholars, realize that a call to scholarship means that the Christian must do even this work as unto the Lord and for his glory.

Yet God has not called all Christians to the life and work of a scholar any more than he has called all to the work of a missionary. While in college obtaining an education, the Christian student equally with his professor must strive to become as effective a scholar as possible. But his ultimate place in life may be far from a university classroom or from the researcher's laboratory or study, for God may not have given him the abilities or even the desire to teach, to do research or to write. He does not call everyone to the same work in life

While granting this, however, we would not wish to adopt the attitude that the Christian, once his formal education has come to an end, may then give up his scholarly attitudes in order to revert to the old imprecise and often humanistic way of thinking which he followed originally. The Christian still has the responsibility of bringing every thought into obedience to Christ. While in college his teachers continually drilled into him the importance of hard work and deep thought, but this does not end as he steps from the academic portals. He must continually wrestle with the same problems but now in different forms, for only as he continues to think along Christian lines about everything, will his Christian life be strong and fruitful. In the true sense of the word he must continue to be a scholar.

What does this mean in actual practice? It means first of all the necessity of maintaining a critical attitude at all times — not a carping attitude which is often common to many Christians — but a carefully analytic approach to all matters, that he may truly understand and evaluate them in the light of his basic Christian faith. When he does this he will be able to see many of the fallacies of the humanistic position: the unwarranted assumptions, the illogical methods and the false conclusions concerning the meaning of this universe in which man lives. In so doing, he will also come to a better understanding of his own position as a Christian.

As the Christian so thinks, he will the better serve Christ in this world, thus fulfilling the words "Thy kingdom come, thy will be done on earth as it is in heaven." This will be the case because he will, as Paul puts it, "have the mind of Christ." Seeing all things in his light he will have the ability to understand more fully and completely God's purpose and work in the world. The resulting thinking and acting on his part will be to the glory of God, the highest objective to which man may strive.

But what of the professional scholar? He above all others must be diligent in his "business, serving the Lord." In this day and age he faces a tremendous challenge which may well cause him to quail and fear. But when he examines closely the challenge presented to him, he finds that the non-Christian on his own basis cannot logically even cast doubt on the Christian's position, let alone demonstrate his philosophy's superiority to the Christian's interpretation. Indeed he has to admit that he secretly accepts "a Christian universe." Consequently, today Christian scholars have a responsibility to devote themselves more fully to their calling in order that they may face and overcome the contemporary humanistic challenge.

APPENDIX

HISTORICAL MATERIALISM: EMPIRICAL OR METAPHYSICAL?

Historical materialism has for nearly a century, if not longer, been regarded by those who accept it as the only key to history which will give "scientific results." Indeed, so widely was this point of view accepted during the twenties and early thirties of the present century, that practically all historical problems whether they related to Greek art, the Reformation or the growth of scientific knowledge were explained in Marxist materialistic categories. Although today this interpretation is perhaps not taken quite so seriously, it still forms the basis whether conscious or unconscious, of many students' interpretations of events, despite those same students' definite rejection of historical materialism itself. It would, therefore, seem to be advisable to see whether it is as infallibly empirical an interpretation as it asserts, or whether it is in truth simply one among a number of immanent "metaphysical" analyses of the historical process.

It is a truism to say that historical materialism in its present form finds its origins in the writings of Marx and Engels. They laid the foundations for later elaboration which have appeared in the writings of various individuals today, perhaps one of the best known being Professor Maurice Dobb of Cambridge University. Besides applying this interpretation to a number of studies, Professor Dobb in 1951 summed up the materialistic "philosophy" in an article in *History*. Although relatively short for such an important subject, the article seems to epitomize this point of view so adequately that in the present discussion, continual reference will be made to it.[1]

---

[1] Dobb, Maurice, "Historical Materialism and the Role of the Economic Factor," *History*, N.S. XXXVI (1951), 1-11.

If there is one basic principal upon which Marx and all his successors have insisted it is that they are, more than anyone else, empirical. Marx in his preface to the second edition of *Capital* stressed this repeatedly, pointing out that while he had employed the Hegelian dialectic as his method of exposition, he had in fact rescued it from the "upside-down" position in which Hegel had unfortunately placed it. In the same vein Dobb in his article stresses that "historical materialism originated in the antithesis" to Hegel's view that every step in the historical process is determined by the "idea" or "conception" of the times. Historical materialists claim that such an interpretation being fundamentally metaphysical, they have turned from it to examine history scientifically and empirically, refusing to permit philosophy, and more especially metaphysics, to influence their interpretations.[2]

Such a point of view naturally appeals to those who have been much impressed with the wonders of applied science and who have come to doubt fine-spun philosophical theories. The historical materialist, refusing to accept any "dogmas," begins his interpretation with the facts empirically discovered. On this basis he very quickly comes to the important conclusion that "the determining element in history is *ultimately* production and reproduction in real life."[3] The economic factor is the most basic of all forces in the historical process. At the same time, however, the historical materialist also believes that the ideas and concepts originally arising out of the economic ground-motive of history, reciprocally influence and so modify, the economic forces. But when all this has been said the economic factor is still ultimate, the "mode of production," the foundation of all history.

---

[2] Dobb, pp. 1 and 2; cf. K. Marx, *The Poverty of Philosophy*, (London, [1936]), pp. 88f.

[3] Engels quoted in Dobb, p. 3; cf. Marx, pp. 92, 93.

This raises the question of the meaning of "the mode of production." Dobb in his article points out that the Marxist interpretation has been frequently misinterpreted by being limited to nothing more than the technology of production. The true position of the historical materialist would seem to be that by this term he means the whole complex of production which includes both the "forces of production" and the "social relations of production."[4] These give rise to all the other phenomena of history, and they in turn exercise a reciprocal influence upon their prime movers.

A question which arises at this point is: How empirical are these conclusions? The problem would seem to be the same as that of the man who desires to determine which comes first, the chicken or the egg. Does the historical materialist in devising the economic interpretation, actually begin with empirical observation, or does he commence by making certain universal assumptions involving the nature of things in general? If he does the latter, can one draw any other conclusion than that his real reasoning finds its starting point in a metaphysic, or more accurately in an act of materialistic "religious" faith?

Before considering the matter further at this point, one must examine carefully the historical materialist's understanding of the process of history. To him, in accordance with his assumption of the fundamental character of the economic factor, the basic drive in history is a dialectical conflict between economic classes, whom one might almost denominate as the "haves" and the "have-nots." As Dobb has stated it: "In this sense divisions between political groups or parties and between ideologies were derivative from the tension within the social relationships of production."[5] It is this dialectical

[4] Dobb, p. 10.

[5] *Ibid.*, p. 10; cf. also K. Marx and F. Engels, "The Communist Manifesto."

conflict which produces all features of culture, thought and civilization. Yet while very certain that this position is the only "empirical" one, Dobb, basing his assertion upon Marx as his final authority, declares: "That the shaping of individuals by their social milieu and of social groups by their relations to the mode of production is a simple formula which can yield a direct answer to every historical problem, no serious Marxist has ever maintained." Moreover, he quotes Engels' statement that the materialist interpretation is a guide for study, not a lever for construction.[6] For this reason while the materialistic interpreter asserts that his economic interpretation of history ultimately explains all historical phenomena, he also admits that the connections between many historical phenomena (e.g., art, religion, etc.) and their basic cause are never empirically verifiable.

Naturally, this again raises the point: Is then historical materialism empirical? The materialist claims to be rigidly scientific, but at the same time allows that he has not been able to demonstrate the link between economic causation and many cultural phenomena. In other words, although he states categorically that there is causal relationship between the economic factor, i.e., the mode of production, and contemporary civilization, when one demands empirical proof of this generalization he acknowledges it to be but an assumption. It would seem that here again, although he claims to accept only the results of scientific investigation, there is behind the materialist a whole series of unconsciously introduced metaphysical ideas. Can one then accept his claim that his position is truly empirical?

This leads to a further step. One of the important characteristics of science is that it is able to project its conclusions into the future to make predictions concerning physical events yet to happen. For instance, Halley was able to predict the time of the reappearance of a com-

[6] Dobb, pp. 7, 8.

et which had already been seen a number of times before. With this "scientific" method can the historical materialist do the same thing?

The answer of Marx and his disciples is an unequivocal affirmative. While Dobb on the other hand, in his article does not specifically touch upon this matter, the implications as we shall see are that prediction is definitely possible. Other historical materialists have, like Marx, carried their theory through to the bitter end, declaring that the inevitable culmination of history will be revolution which will produce the classless society. They are thus, on the basis of the scientific study of the past, able to predict a future revolution, and not content with that, to state what will be the state of affairs after the revolution.[7]

Such a conclusion, however, seems to be hardly scientific. A true revolution, by its very nature, tears up the old in order to introduce something principally new. True there have usually been connections between the pre-revolutionary and the post-revolutionary state of affairs, as far as *historical* revolutions are known. But these upheavals according to Marx, have all been only partial. The proletarian revolution, on the other hand, will be the revolution to end all revolutions. It will be total. Now, apart from the question of how he is able to predict at all on the basis of a study of the past, there is the question of how one may prophesy from the pre-revolutionary situation, what will be the state of affairs after the completion of the revolution. To this query there seems to be hardly a "scientific" answer, rather it seems to be based upon metaphysical assumptions, the very existence of which Dobb, Marx and all other historical materialists are constrained to deny.

[7] "Communist Manifesto"; F. Engels, *Socialism Utopian and Scientific* (New York, 1935), pp. 69ff.

This suspicion that Dobb, Engels, Marx and other historical materialists actually presuppose a metaphysical system behind history is borne out by their denials of ultimate historical relativism. Dobb is very insistent upon this, rejecting any idea that his views are really only a "sociology of knowledge," and there are both "bourgeois" and "proletarian" truths about history. For all this school's rejection of relativism, however, one cannot but find its "absolutism" a little difficult to swallow. If the "mode of production" ultimately determines all forms of human society and thought, as the mode of production changes so must thought change and with it, even historical materialism. Moreover, it would seem that the views of different social classes would vary according to the current mode of production at different times. While everyone might be considered to be out of step except the proletariat, one must realize that even the proletariat's economic position changes, bringing alterations in its "world view." This would be particularly true once the ultimate social revolution had taken place. Consequently even historical materialism would seem to have been relativized and with it all and every interpretation of history.

As Dobb has pointed out, such a conclusion is as far from the desires of the materialists as it could be. Wherever and whenever they write they sound like the prophets of the Old Testament in their assurance, the fundamental difference being that while the prophets always prefaced their words with "Thus saith the Lord," Dobb and others usually commence by quoting Marx, or assume the self-evident character of their basic materialistic assumption. The opening sentence of part three of Engels' *Socialism Utopian and Scientific* brings this out clearly: "The materialist conception of history starts from the proposition that the production of the means to support human life, and, next to production, the exchange of things produced, is the basis of all social structure. . . ." Assuming the absolute validity of such a premise, it is hardly surprising that Dobb, to refute the charge of relativism, should hold all interpretations of history to have some elements of "truth" in them, those that are more scientifically materialistic being closer to "absolute truth" than those that are less scientific. "Absolute truth was not a Kantian unknowable, even if it could never be reached at any finite point in the historical process: it could be approached asymptotically, and criteria existed by which one could speak about being nearer to it or more remote."

While this sounds quite plausible, one is still left in something of a quandary, since on the basis of historical materialism, it is rather difficult to discuss "absolute truth." What is it? Presumably it has certain characteristics by which it may be known, but how one may discover these characteristics in the womb of ultimate materialism is not stated. Indeed, at this point there seems to be another basic inconsistency in the whole system of thought. The historical materialist knows only individual historical "facts," which are individual entities without connection. Of course he will claim that there are connections but without any basic principles of unity which he knows "scientifically," they are in truth not related. Any principle of coherence which he may attempt to adopt is purely the concoction of his own "materialistically" determined mind. This gives no more than a working hypothesis, and certainly not "absolute truth."

Yet such a suggestion as this by no means satisfies the historical materialists. They talk as though there is an absolute principle of coherence in and over history. Dobb, for instance, in the sentence quoted above apparently accepts the idea of absolute truth, and Marx, although he may not have used the term, still presupposed

[8] Dobb, p. 9.

the absoluteness of the dialectical movement of history towards a classless society. This would seem to be in direct conflict with their denial of everything but the facts of the material universe.

To this charge of innate contradiction and of a hidden metaphysic the historical materialist may well reply that he and his fellows are not talking of an "idea" in the sense of Hegel, but merely of the observed process in nature and history. True, but when they begin to make this process absolute, and on the basis of its absolutism to predict the future, it would seem to be more than a mere hypothesis. Moreover, their firm belief that although unknown until the nineteenth century, this process has always been going on, points to its existence as something which is more than a mere haphazard accident. Since it is innate in nature and history it would seem to be eternally absolute.[9]

If this be the case, it would seem that this "absolute truth" is not subject to history itself, whose very essence is, according to the dialectical materialist, the dialectical movement of change. No matter what happens in history, the same "absolute truth" is always there as a supra-historical entity, unaffected by the laws of movement. Thus the historical materialists claim that his "absolute truth" is only the observed process of nature seems hardly to fit the case. He has assumed in truth the existence of a metaphysical "idea" which dwells in a realm outside of history.

At this point he is unable to stop, for he has already laid great stress upon the existence of this "idea," this "absolute truth" or whatever one may call it, in history. Indeed it is the very life blood of history, working itself out through economic evolution and social conflict, with the end result that history is made to conform to it. If one looks closely at this idea it is hard to escape the conviction that once again Hegel has appeared, albeit in a

[9] Marx, *The Poverty of Philosophy*, pp. 97f., 103f.

somewhat unexpected guise. Although Marx, Engels and their cohorts have always been very scornful of Hegel, it looks as though he has infiltrated their lines as a metaphysical fifth column.

At this point another question arises. If this absolute "idea" or "truth" does mold history to its pattern, how does it do so? It is above history and yet within it, but by what means are the two connected? How is it that history with all its change and movement continues to follow out this predetermined pattern which will eventually lead to the classless society? To this the historical materialist returns no answer. Rejecting, of course, anything like a doctrine of creation or a pantheistic-idealistic philosophy, he does not bother to solve this very crucial problem. Hardly a scientific approach!

The Knowledge of His Truth

The reason for this lacuna in his reasoning may of course come from the difficulty of proving that he may know the criteria whereby one may even obtain a glimpse of his "absolute truth." Or, to put the matter in the form of a question: How does he know that the dialectical process is fundamental to history, and how does he know that it is going to bring in the good, the true and the beautiful classless society? True, he claims that he has discovered this by "historical research." But out of historical research what does he bring forth? It would seem that he is able to produce only facts not necessarily connected, which leave him with no real scientific knowledge, and certainly with no certainty or assurance that the "absolute truth" will be eventually worked out in history.

To understand the facts, the historical materialist must know their relationships. Moreover, to make valid generalizations concerning the whole process of history, of which he is a part, he must know all their relationships, otherwise his absolute generalizations and his absolute certainties concerning the basic idea or process of history must fall to the ground. This is particularly true when the historian ceases to be a historian and turns prophet. To make predictions on the basis of his knowledge of past history, he projects his ideas into the area of the non-factual by stating what will happen after the proletarian revolution. Such a point of view would be consistent with the faith of the Old Testament prophets, but it is hardly appropriate for materialists who deny the existence of a god, and so fundamentally reject any possibility of a valid pre-interpretation of anything in the universe. Where then does the historical materialist obtain his knowledge? What is the origin of his omniscence? To these queries he gives no adequate answer.

When one attempts to analyze his ideas, however, one quickly comes to realize that his views are again dependent upon a series of basic assumptions. To establish his epistemology he begins with the idea of a coherent universe in which everything is related. Only on this ground could Dobb, for instance, assume that the method of production determines the contemporary religion, art and philosophy, for he himself admits that such a view cannot be substantiated from the historical facts. To carry the matter a little further, this assumption also seems to be at the root of his idea of "absolute truth" for he feels that all thought can approach in some way or other within hailing distance of the truth, even though it may fall far short of it. It is for this reason that, while denying the possibility of divine revelation concerning reality, he holds very strongly to the ability of man, and in particular the historian, to know truth and to know the idea behind the whole historical development. His position rests upon the two assumptions of "a coherent universe" and "absolute truth," neither of which he has proved or seems able to prove.

How, therefore, does he know all this? It would seem to be that he has taken his presuppositions, applied them to the facts and produced his results. In other words, despite the tremendous paraphernalia of historical scholarship, and despite the importance of much of the work which the historical materialist has accomplished, his system rests not upon a scientifically empirically developed system of thought, but on a process of rationalization which has deduced certain consequences from basic presuppositions and has then fitted the facts into the logically derived theories. The results of this process can hardly be called scientific. In actual truth he can have no certainty that his knowledge of either "the absolute truth" beyond history, or its relationship to history has any validity whatsoever. Once again he ends up with an ultimate contradiction between what he claims to do and what he actually does. His theory of knowledge cannot bear the weight of what he claims is the nature of reality.

The Ethical Problem

There is, however, one more point which must be made, and this relates to the matter of ethics. Although Marx and all his followers are strong on the fact that they are purely scientific and that everything is ultimately determined by the natural dialectic of the economic and social struggle, there is always a strongly ethical tone to their writing. There is forever the condemnation of the exploiters of the proletariat which finds its classic expression in the *Communist Manifesto*. This tone is not merely a mid-nineteenth century vestigial remain, but is essential to the whole pattern of the historical materialist's thought. Since the workers of the world have nothing to lose but their chains, they should unite to throw off the horrible bondage under which they suffer. Revolution becomes a moral responsibility upon which men turn their backs at their peril.

This attitude poses a rather important problem. On the basis of the historical materialist's acknowledged presuppositions how is it possible for there to be any moral, any good or bad, acts? What is the difference between good and bad; and whence does knowledge of them come? But there is also another side to this problem. Even admitting that "good" and "bad" do exist as valid differences, since society is fundamentally determined by purely materialistic forces outside the individual, how is the latter responsible for what he does? Why condemn the bourgeoisie for its exploitation of the proletariat, when the bourgeoisie itself is simply the product of the dialectical process of economic evolution? The historical materialist has to face the problem of whether or not there is such a thing as human responsibility, and if there is, of its significance.

As one reads Marx and his disciples one cannot but gather that one's attitude to the proletariat is a rule by which one's morality is measured. Acts which favor and help the proletariat are good, those which are against them and to their disadvantage are bad. This is true, however, only on a "long term basis," for Marx and others have pointed out that sometimes one might take actions which are ostensibly for the welfare of the proletariat but which in the end do not help them on towards the great revolution. For this reason he had no love for liberals who sought the reform but not the complete overthrow of the capitalistic system. The motive, therefore, as well as the act itself one must take into account if one is truly to judge its ethical status.

Here again "absolute truth" raises its head. "The idea" which determines the course of history, driving it on to the classless society, seems to be really the ultimate standard of action. It is this idea which the historical materialist uses as his means of criticizing history, societies and individuals, relegating them to "the good" or "the bad." Moreover, it is on the basis of this idea that he proclaims ultimately the "rightness" of the eventual appearance of the classless society.

While this may sound very logical, one cannot help asking the question: by what authority is the idea of the welfare of the proletariat declared to be "the good"? Does it derive from the Christian: blessed are the poor (Lk. 6: 20f.)? Or does it come from the thinking of Jeremy Bentham and James Mill? The historical materialist does not say. It is apparently merely his decision and that of other historical materialists, that the welfare of the proletariat should be the primary concern of everyone, and is the highest end and objective of historical development.

When one states such a position, he is forced back to the fact that the idea of the "good" is entirely a human creation, arising out of the social process caused by the dialectic of economic development. It would seem, therefore, that ethics at this point become purely relative. They are nothing more than the standards of a certain form of economic and social society which may change with the mode of production. Yet in the face of this his own interpretation, the historical materialist still lays down the "idea" of the welfare of the proletariat and progress to the classless society, as being the objective for which every right thinking person should work. Here, as in the case of his metaphysics and his epistemology, there seems to be a fundamental contradiction.

The Presuppositions of Historical Materialism

Thus if one attempts to make an analysis of the dogmatic statements of the historical materialist, he inevitably finds that the latter's claims to scientific and empirical accuracy and certitude are in no way consistent with his basic presuppositions. While declaring himself to be free of philosophical ideas, he actually turns up with an assumed metaphysics, epistemology and ethics, at the core of which is the basic belief in a pattern of history which finds its expression in the dialectical movement of time towards the classless society.

Yet, as noted above, while assuming such an array of philosophical constructions, he flaty denies that he makes them. He declares that the economic factor, its study and measurement, is the only real force which interests him, for it is the only real motive of history. He is scientific and opposed to such unscientific practices as the making of assumptions, but at the same time he covertly adopts them and uses them for his own purposes. One sometimes wonders whom he thinks he is fooling.

One may, however, carry this criticism even further. If for the sake of argument, one admits the truth of the historical materialist's position, one is obliged to ask by what right he makes any generalizations particularly concerning that most difficult of all studies, history. Moreover, on what basis can he make generalizations about anything scientific, since if there is no existence but material, no knowledge but that derived from history, and no moral imperative except that which comes from a certain mode of production at a certain point in time and space, ultimate chance would seem to rule? It would thus appear that historical materialism destroys itself by its own profession. It must either retire into the corner and make no statements about anything, or it must begin by assuming a whole complex of reality behind the material universe, the understanding of which must be obtained by some other means than empirical observation and measurement.

In this dilemma the historical materialist is not alone, for it would seem that all immanent systems of philosophy have the same difficulty. Making man the creator of the system of explanation, they are unable to rise above the limitations of the relativism of history. Even if they attempt to remain in this completely relativistic situation, they still have their problems, for once they begin to make universal judgments they are presupposing a state of affairs which can hardly be said to find its ultimate proof in a small segment of reality, or even of history. They are taking for granted that there is a fundamental coherence in the universe, by which it is possible to interpret reality, and that there is meaning to history which is above and beyond the changing patterns of historical events. In other words, the philosopher of history is forced to assume a supra-historical reality, if he is to make any statements about history as a whole.

Such an assumed supra-historical reality can perhaps be termed the philosopher's religion. It is his basic standpoint from which he begins all his thinking, and it is thus supra-theoretical, accepted by an intuitive faith. The question then arises as to whether or not this faith is valid—does it make sense of the universe, and in this particular case, the process of history? Here is the real crux of the whole question of historical materialism. As we have seen, this philosophy of history accepts on faith a supra-theoretical starting point which, almost immediately afterwards, in order to maintain its desired materialism, it must perforce deny. This hardly makes for a logical or a scientific philosophy of history, and it will hardly therefore present an explanation of historical events which one may regard as being valid.

The Christian Alternative

In the light of the failure of historical materalism to be truly scientific, is there any answer to this riddle of history? From the human point of view, one might well answer in the negative, for how can man, within time and subject to time, discover a point of vantage from which he is able to see history as a whole and so derive an understanding of its pattern and its meaning?

To such a question neither materialistic science nor idealistic philosophy provides anything but guesses for an answer. It is at this point that Christianity comes in, offering a realistic, self-consistent interpretation which gives meaning to history and so to human action.

The basic reason for stating that Christianity can solve this ever present problem is, that of all interpretations of history it alone accepts frankly man's inability by himself to interpret history. Even the historian who holds that history is but the operation of chance is inconsistent in making a general interpretative statement. The Christian, on the other hand, believes that general statements and judgments may be made concerning history because there is a supra-historical interpreter who has made a prehistorical interpretation. The interpreter is the sovereign triune God, the creator, upholder and ruler of the universe who "does all things according to the counsel of his own will" (Eph. 1: 11).

At the same time the Christian knows only too well that men do not wish to accept such a solution to the problem. They usually prefer to have chance rather than the sovereign God as the final arbiter of history. At this the Christian can feel no surprise, for believing that man is a morally responsible being, he is also sure that man desires to assert himself in history by refusing God his true glory. Therefore, man turns himself away from God, the result being sin and evil in history. But this evil is not the economic determination of the historical materialist; rather it is the evil arising out of the wilful disobedience of the rebellious creature who refuses to worship the Creator, and so seeks for a simple, unitary and immanent explanation for all historical development.

Man's wilfulness and sin can have only one result: blindness. Consequently although by God's favor the non-Christian may discover much concerning the immediate connections of historical facts, when he comes to making general statements, or even to proving that he has the ability to uncover the immediate facts and their relations in history, he lands in complete inconsistency. The Christian would hold, however, that man's rejection of God as the ultimate interpreter will be changed to acceptance only by God's gracious act of giving man sight. When he is then able to see properly, he will understand the truth of the Christian position.

Man even before he sinned needed to have revealed to him the meaning and significance of history, but since sin and disobediance has entered into creation man needs more than revelation. He needs redemption, which will open his eyes and turn him back to the true faith and obedience. This the Christian believes has come in history through God's self-revelation in his redemptive action culminating in the incarnation, death and resurrection of the Son, all of which is recorded in the Scriptures of the Old and New Testaments. Thus the Word, both living and written, gives men the true explanation and understanding of the meaning of history.

The Christian, therefore, standing in the midst of history, and realizing that to interpret history one must always commence with certain supra-theoretical assumptions, begins with an acceptance of the Gospel and all it means, while over against him stands the non-Christian endeavoring from the facts of history to discover its ultimate meaning. For the non-Christian the end result is always the same as that to which the historical materialist has come: inconsistency and self-destruction. For the Christian, however, beginning with the revelation of the sovereign God, there is no inconsistency, nor is there any destruction of history. Although he realizes that he cannot know everything about history, he believes that it is coherent in God's purpose of which he can comprehend at least a small part. Thus when he talks of an understanding of history as a whole, he does so not on the basis of the accumulation of historical data, but ultimately on that of the revealed counsel of God. In this he is consistent and can deal with all historical facts as they come, knowing that they are God's historical revelation of himself.

Reid

Christianity and Scholarship.